AF663743

DAYS OF THE APOCALYPSE

THE TIMES OF THE END

DAYS OF THE APOCALYPSE

THE TIMES OF THE END

SANJAY MALWE

Qurate
quratebooks.com
Because everyone has a story to tell

THE TIMES OF THE END

Sanjay Malwe

Published by Qurate Books Pvt Ltd.

© Sanjay Malwe

All rights reserved

All rights reserved. No part of this publication may be reproduced, stored in a retrieval system or transmitted in any form or by any means, electronic, mechanical, photocopying, recording or otherwise, without the prior permission of the author or publisher.

First Published in 2022

ISBN: 978-93-94600-26-3

Qurate Books Pvt. Ltd.
Goa 403523, India
www.quratebooks.com
Tel: 1800-210-6527
Email: info@quratebooks.com

Cover Designed by: Vandana Giby

FORWARD

If I am asked this question - how would you describe Sanjay Malwe in one sentence?

I would say, "His passion to learn and teach God's word is impeccable and is his utmost purpose in life."

As a pastor we as a congregation have not just been blessed and encouraged by his teaching but by also seeing him practice what he teaches and believes.

He is very compassionate and a generous leader which reflects in his secondary passion to teach the word of God and to support mercy ministries.

Xavier Selvan
Pastor - Healing Nations Church
CEO - Sahaara Charitable Society

A committed Christian, a dedicated Bible student and a great teacher of the Word of God - that is what always comes to my mind about Sanjay Malwe, the author of this Book.

Since the last so many years, he has conducted Bible studies on various topics like "The End Times", "The book of Revelation" and many books of the Bible on different occasions.

He has been highly appreciated in his style of delivery, and his teaching skills.

He has spent many hours researching and preparing the text of what is before you.

Gissy Jacob John

CONTENTS

1. The Bible - A historical record and revelation of the future. 9

2. World Empires – Israel the prophetic clock....17

3. Israel fails to recognize the Messiah....33

4. Jesus summarizes the last days 45

5. The Olivet discourse and "The book of Revelation" 55

6. The unholy alliance & the coalition of The "Beasts of Revelation"....71

7. Identifying the Anti-Christ....91

8. The city of Babylon and the Scarlet Beast 107

9. The future battles against Israel....119

10. The King returns....133

CHAPTER 1

THE BIBLE

A historical record and revelation of the future.

WHY DO WE NEED TO STUDY THE END TIMES?

JESUS IS COMING SOON! This is something many of us have heard over and over so much so it has become a cliché of sorts in Christian circles. Can we just write it off as Christian jingoism?

Does not the Word of God state, that the *Day* and the *Hour* is not known? After all there are so many charlatans out there predicting the end times and so many of these predictions regarding the date of the Lord's return have failed. Many genuine Christians have been disappointed when these predictions failed. Some have just turned away from all teachings on the topic of the Lord's return.

I decided to dig deeper into the Bible to understand what the Bible said about this. So, I framed the following questions.

Is the Day and Hour unknown? The answer is a definite YES.

Should we therefore not concern ourselves about the end times and endeavor just to be good Christians in our day?
The answer is a resounding NO!

The scriptures encourage us to look forward to the return of the Lord. In the parable of the ten virgins, the bridegroom took a long time to come. He suddenly returned in the dead of the night to take His bride away. Jesus warned the Church to be ALERT. In fact, we are repeatedly cautioned that we should be on our guard and not become careless and unwary. We are constantly encouraged to look forward to "the day" of the Lord's return and understand the signs of the times.

LUKE 12:54-58

And He was also saying to the crowds, "When you see a cloud rising in the west, immediately you say, 'A shower is coming,' and so it turns out. And when you see a south wind blowing, you say, 'It will be a hot day,' and it turns out that way. You hypocrites! You know how to analyze the appearance of the earth and the sky, but why do you not analyze this present time?

WHY SHOULD I BELIEVE BIBLE PROPHECY?

One aspect that really sets the Bible apart from other religious texts is the prophetic nature of the book. Almost a third of the Bible is prophetic. God knows the past as well as the future.

The Bible keeps a record of history and unveils the future. It has a track record of a hundred percent accuracy in past prophecies. Prophecies that have already been fulfilled include the history of Israel.

Even before they entered the promised land, God had revealed through the prophet Moses, every detail of the future of Israel. He had also announced in advance their failure to keep their part of the covenant and the subsequent results for disobedience. (Deuteronomy 28)

The Bible records over 300 prophecies about the coming of the Messiah, His miraculous birth, His death and resurrection. Every prophecy has been fulfilled exactly as predicted.

More recently the rebirth of the nation of Israel, had been prophesied by Old Testament prophets and by Jesus. There are no grey areas, nothing left to speculation. The prophecies were clearly stated and happened exactly as they were described.

Looking at the world around us with regards to the abuse of the earth's resources, the total breakdown of personal morality and the decadence of society, it is clear that we are in the final days of this age. Unless God intervenes soon, mankind will destroy itself completely.

If we were to ask Bible believing Christians about the "coming of Jesus" there will be mixed answers to the same question. Some believe that it is an event which is very near and we do not have much time. Some are of the opinion that, as we do not know when He would come, it is better not to speculate. Some take the warnings in the "book of Revelation" very earnestly while others are almost reluctant to venture near this book.

But all agree that the word of God is true and therefore must be taken seriously.

ISAIAH 46:9-10

"Remember the former things long past,
For I am God, and there is no other;
I am God, and there is no one like Me,
Declaring the end from the beginning,
And from ancient times things which have not been done,
Saying, 'My purpose will be established,
And I will accomplish all My good pleasure';

THE EARLY HISTORY OF MAN

The Bible gives an accurate account of the creation of the earth along with the heavens which includes the entire galaxy. It records the creation of Man along with all animals and the creatures of the sea.

It also records the rebellion of man and the consequences that would arise as a result. The earth as well as all of mankind along with the entire creation on the earth would then spiral downward towards death.

But through the opening pages of the Bible, we also get a glimpse of the redemption plan that God would initiate through the coming of Jesus.

The Bible records the downward spiral of mankind into sin, with such a torrent of evil, that God would have to send a catastrophic flood that would wipe out all mankind. Only Noah and his family survived.

Even as mankind moved on after the flood, the heart of man was imprinted with a rebellious nature and this brought about the incident of the "Tower of Babel". After this incident, God confused the language of the people and people began to move in groups to different parts of the then undivided land mass.

ABRAHAM AND THE NATION OF ISRAEL

This continued for around 2000 years. God chose a man named Abraham and promised him and his descendants a land which is fondly called "The Promised Land". The present-day nation of Israel is only a small portion of the vast land promised to Abraham's descendants.

The descendants of Abraham flourished and grew in number. After staying in Egypt, they eventually became slaves in the land. However, they were granted freedom by God in a dramatic way and later they re-occupied the Promised Land.

A MIXED BAG:

Israel's experience was a mixed bag in the land of promise. After gaining victory and possessing the land through the leadership of many Judges and Prophets, they seemed to stagger in cycles of rebellion, defeat, repentance and restoration for almost 500 years.

They were then ruled for almost another 500 years by kings under whom the nation was divided into two parts; the southern kingdom of Judah and the northern kingdom of Israel.

When Israel chose to be ruled by kings, this move brought about disaster upon the northern kingdom of Israel which comprised of ten tribes.

This kingdom went into captivity into Assyria and the ten tribes were dispersed into the nations in the year 722 B.C.

The southern kingdom of Judah continued for almost another 150 years but ultimately was also conquered by the kingdom of Babylon in 607 B.C.

BACK FROM CAPTIVITY TO THE COMING OF THE MESSIAH

Back from captivity, the Israelites had learned the lesson that God kept His promises as well as took action to bring His people from straying. The people of Israel had come back to the land of promise and were guided by the High Priests for almost another 500 years.

In line with the prophecies given by the prophets, the "Son of God" came down as the "Son of Man" to redeem not only the people of Israel but all of mankind.

History itself is divided in time with the coming of the Messiah. He was not recognized by His own people who rejected Him and turned Him over to be crucified. Once again, the Jews had missed the opportunity of being reconciled to God and because of their rejection of the Messiah; the city of Jerusalem and the Nation of Israel would once again become desolate.

THE PROPHETIC WARNINGS

Time and again the people of Israel had messed up their call. They were to be a special people of God. God Himself had chosen them and wanted them to be a light to the world. Instead, their disobedience to the commands of God, and their consistent failure to heed to the warnings of the Prophets sent by God, would cause their downfall.

The prophets had encouraged the people that God would always keep His part of the Covenant. But He also expected Israel to keep their part. He had also warned them many times that their consistent disobedience would lead to dire consequences. They had been warned in advance about the captivity by the Assyrians as well as the Babylonians.

They had been given sufficient details of the coming of the Messiah. Yet they had not recognized the Messiah when He walked among them.

THE FUTURE "RETURN OF THE KING"

The Bible is a unique book because it not only records the past but also accurately predicts the future course of events.

The Old Testament predicted in great detail the coming of Jesus. His death on the cross would become the ultimate display of the love of God in forgiving the sins of man through faith in His Son. The prophets had accurately predicted every aspect of the life of the Messiah.

- His nature and His Deity.
- His supernatural birth.
- The location of His birth
- The time of His arrival
- The life He would live.
- The way that the Messiah would teach the word of God.
- His death, burial and resurrection.

The Bible has accurately predicted the rise and fall of many of the world's greatest empires.

It goes into great detail of the signs that would occur and the events that would dominate the world. It also gives us insight with detail the end time events that will occur just prior to the return of Jesus.

The Bible gives us a vivid picture of the Kingdom of God that will be established on the earth.

The Bible declares that finally mankind will have a king, who is not only all powerful, but is righteous and just. He will reign over the nations and bring peace on the earth. He will also restore the earth and end violence not only among men but also among all of God's creation

THE JEWS DID NOT RECOGNIZE THE TIME OF THEIR VISITATION

Although the Lord had warned His people through the prophets and the Jews had the scriptures, they did not recognize the time of the visitation of the Messiah.

Jesus wept over the city of Jerusalem when they had rejected Him. The city would be left desolate and the Jews would face eviction from the Promised Land. If they had only searched and understood the scriptures, their history would have been different.

LUKE 19:40-45

When He approached Jerusalem, He saw the city and wept over it, saying,

"If you had known in this day, even you, the things which make for peace! But now they have been hidden from your eyes. For the days will come upon you when your enemies will throw up a barricade against you, and surround you and hem you in on every side, and they will level you to the ground and your children within you, and they will not leave in you one stone upon another, because you did not recognize the time of your visitation."

It is now around 2000 years since the Church era began. God has provided sufficient details for us to know the season of His return. We may not know the exact day and hour, but we do know the season. Just as we know that the monsoon season begins in the month of June in Mumbai every year. We may not know the exact day when it will begin to rain. But we do know the season.

In the same way, we may not know the exact date of His return. But as we study the Scriptures and seek the return of the Lord, we can avoid the mistake that the Jewish leadership made. The return of the Messiah is very near and we can recognize the season of His coming.

ROMANS 13:12

The night is nearly over; the day is almost here. So let us put aside the deeds of darkness and put on the armor of light.

CHAPTER 2

WORLD EMPIRES

Israel the prophetic clock

The whole creation speaks about the power and the attributes of God. It declares His authority and wisdom through His handiwork. From the complexity of the simplest cells in our bodies, to the power that each atom holds; to the vastness of the galaxies, all point to the awesome glory of God.

But God delights the most in mankind. He speaks to man not only as God Almighty, but also as a father and friend. The Lord has spoken throughout history. In the past He spoke through the Prophets but He finally spoke through His Son Jesus.

THE UNVEILING OF HISTORY IN THE BOOK OF DANIEL

Through the prophet Daniel, God gave an outline of the history of the world, while keeping the nation of Israel as the point of reference. It is vital that we remember that the nation of Israel plays a key role in understanding the times that we live in.

In fact, Israel can be seen as a prophetic clock by which we can know time.

DANIEL 2:20-21

Let the name of God be blessed forever and ever,
For wisdom and power belongs to Him.
"It is He who changes the times and the epochs;
He removes kings and establishes kings;
He gives wisdom to wise men
And knowledge to men of understanding.

In the 2nd chapter of the book of Daniel, king Nebuchadnezzar has a dream that troubles Him. No one is able to reveal to the king his dream or give an interpretation of the dream except Daniel.

This dream of Nebuchadnezzar in the 2nd chapter of Daniel as well as dream that Daniel has in chapter 7 regarding the four beasts, are the foundations on which we understand biblical eschatology.

THE STATUE OF NEBUCHADNEZZAR'S DREAM

THE KING'S DREAM - DANIEL 2:31-45

"You, O king, were looking and behold, there was a single great statue; that statue, which was large and of extraordinary splendor, was standing in front of you, and its appearance was awesome.

The head of that statue was made of fine gold, its breast and its arms of silver, its belly and its thighs of bronze, its legs of iron, its feet partly of iron and partly of clay. You continued looking until a stone was cut out without hands, and it struck the statue on its feet of iron and clay and crushed them. Then the iron, the clay, the bronze, the silver and the gold were crushed all at the same time and became like chaff from the summer threshing floors; and the wind carried them away so that not a trace of them was found. But the stone that struck the statue became a great mountain and filled the whole earth.

The Israelites were warned against idolatry and from forsaking the commands of God.

For hundreds of years, God had sent warning after warning through the prophets. God had finally taken them to task. The people of Judah were now exiled in Babylon by king Nebuchadnezzar. Though God punished the nation, they were not forgotten by Him.

God is not only the ruler of Israel but of the whole earth. While in captivity in Babylon, God gave king Nebuchadnezzar a dream. Through this dream given to a pagan king, God had given the blue print for the future. King Nebuchadnezzar was unable to understand the dream.

Daniel who was one of the Jewish exiles however was able to interpret the dream.

1. The head of gold
2. The chest and arms of silver
3. The belly and thighs of bronze
4. The legs of iron
5. The feet partly of iron and partly of clay
6. The stone breaking the statue and becoming a mountain

BABYLON THE FIRST KINGDOM

As we can see, each part of this statue the king saw in his dream represents an actual kingdom.

Accordingly, through the dream, God revealed, the Kingdom of Babylon, was the first kingdom which would rule over the region of Israel and was represented by the head of Gold. This kingdom of Babylon was in power from 606 B.C. to 539 B.C.

MEDO-PERSIA

After a reign of 67 years, the Babylonian Empire was overthrown by the kingdom of the Medes and the Persians. The Medo-Persian monarchy lasted 208 years, from 539 B.C. to 331 B.C.

GREECE

Historic records confirm that in 331 B.C. the Greek armies destroyed the last Persian king during the famous Battle of Arbela. The Greeks saw victory under the powerful and young king Alexander the Great. The Greek Empire was then established. Its rule actually covered far more territories than the two previous kingdoms. The reign of the Greek Empire of Alexander lasted 163 years, from 331 B.C. to 168 B.C.

ROME

In 168 B.C., it was the Roman Empire's turn to enact its supreme rule upon the region. Prophetically speaking, iron perfectly symbolizes this kingdom: its military strength and discipline, its domination over many conquered nations, its laws imposed on all people far and wide. Every aspect of this nation was like the strength and endurance of iron.

The Roman Empire divided into East and West.

This western part of the kingdom continued until 476 A.D.

The Eastern wing (Byzantine) continued till 1453 A.D.

The Capital of the Byzantine Empire was Constantinople which has been renamed as Istanbul which is in modern day Turkey.

THE FEET OF CLAY

Then there will be a fourth kingdom as strong as iron; inasmuch as iron crushes and shatters all things, so, like iron that breaks in pieces, it will crush and break all these in pieces. In that you saw the feet and toes, partly of potter's clay and partly of iron, it will be a divided kingdom; but it will have in it the toughness of iron, inasmuch as you saw the iron mixed with common clay. As the toes of the feet were partly of iron and partly of pottery, so some of the kingdom will be strong and part of it will be brittle.

The feet of clay are made partly of iron and partly of clay. The feet have ten toes. These are ten kings and in the time of these ten kings the God of Heaven will set up a kingdom that can never be destroyed. There will be no other kingdoms after this kingdom arrives. So, it is very important for us to identify these ten kings.

There is something very interesting about the feet and the scripture that follows.

DANIEL CH 2:43

And in that you saw the iron mixed with common clay, they will combine with one another in the seed of men; but they will not adhere to one another, even as iron does not combine with pottery.

What is this mixture and why does the Bible talk about mixing with the seed of men?

Who or what mixes with the seed of men?

There is one period mentioned in the bible in the 6th chapter of Genesis that we come across a similar situation. In this passage the Bible records a period of time when the fallen angels began to have sexual relationships with human beings. This brought about children who were a hybrid of semi human beings. Immorality and wickedness sky rocketed and God had to send the great flood during the time of Noah because mankind had become completely depraved.

GENESIS 6: 1-4

Now it came about, when men began to multiply on the face of the land, and daughters were born to them, that the sons of God saw that the daughters of men were beautiful; and they took wives for themselves, whomever they chose. Then the LORD said, "My Spirit shall not strive with man forever, because he also is flesh; nevertheless, his days shall be one hundred and twenty years." The Nephilim were on the earth in those days, and also afterward, when the sons of God came in to the daughters of men, and they bore children to them. Those were the mighty men who were of old, men of renown.

This alludes to the reality that in the last days, during the time of the ten kings, there would be a situation where once again the fallen angels begin to play an active role in world events. Could this refer to a situation in the future when the armies of the earth would be led by an evil being from the supernatural world?

THE KINGDOMS THAT RULED AFTER THE FALL OF ROME

If the Eastern part of the Roman Empire was defeated in 1453 A.D., then what happened to the other kingdoms that followed and ruled over the area of Israel?

The answer is very simple.

The Byzantine Empire was overtaken by Islamic kings who were then consolidated into the Ottoman Empire. The Ottoman Empire continued to control the area until they were defeated in World War 1 in the year 1917 A.D. and the area came under the control of the British Empire.

Since the Bible keeps the nation of Israel as the point of reference, it is important to note that the nation of Israel was under the control of the Romans in the 1st Century. The Romans destroyed the Jewish temple and made Jerusalem desolate in 70 A.D. The Jews were slaughtered and most were sold off as slaves and sent to other parts of the Roman Empire.

The Jews were forbidden to enter Jerusalem in 135 A.D. by the Romans, who then named the area of present-day Israel as Palestine. For almost 2000 years the Jews had no nation and no place in the Promised Land.

The clock had stopped ticking. We no longer had a point of reference.

Then in 1948, the nation of Israel was miraculously re-established.

Now that there is a modern nation of Israel with established boundaries, the clock has once again begun to tick. From the time that Israel was established and recognized as a nation, they have been under threat and have been fighting for survival.

We are now in the time when the ten kings will show up and their agenda will be to destroy Israel.

THE DIVINE KINGDOM

In the latter part of his dream, Nebuchadnezzar sees a rock that was cut without hands. This rock strikes at the feet of iron and clay and crushes them. The entire statue is also crushed and becomes like chaff.

The stone that struck the statue becomes a great mountain and fills the whole earth.

In the days of those kings the God of heaven will set up a kingdom which will never be destroyed, and that kingdom will not be left for another people; it will crush and put an end to all these kingdoms, but it will itself endure forever. Inasmuch as you saw that a stone was cut out of the mountain without hands and that it crushed the iron, the bronze, the clay, the silver and the gold, the great God has made known to the king what will take place in the future; so the dream is true and its interpretation is trustworthy."

The Stone represents the kingdom of heaven which will be established with great power.

The kingdoms of the earth will be utterly destroyed. The Rock becomes a mountain and fills the whole earth. Now God's kingdom will be established in the whole world. The kingdoms of the world will become the kingdom of our God. The prayer that Jesus taught His disciples to pray will be answered completely.

"Let your kingdom come
Let your will be done on earth as it is in heaven."

And he who falls on this stone will be broken to pieces; but on whomever it falls, it will scatter him like dust." **Matthew 21:44**

THE VISION OF THE FOUR BEASTS

While Daniel was still in captivity in Babylon, he had been blessed by God. The Lord had raised him to be the second highest authority in the kingdom of Nebuchadnezzar. Nebuchadnezzar's grandson Belshazzar now ruled over the kingdom of Babylon.

In the 1st year Belshazzar reign, Daniel saw a dream and visions as he lay on his bed. This dream contained four Beasts that arose from the Sea. This Sea was the Mediterranean Sea and the Beasts were four kingdoms that would arise in this region starting with the kingdom of Babylon.

DANIEL 7:1-3

In the first year of Belshazzar king of Babylon Daniel saw a dream and visions in his mind as he lay on his bed; then he wrote the dream down and related the following summary of it.

Daniel said, "I was looking in my vision by night, and behold, the four winds of heaven were stirring up the great sea. And four great beasts were coming up from the sea, different from one another.

WHO ARE THE FOUR BEASTS? DANIEL 7:17

'These great beasts, which are four in numbers, are four kings who will arise from the earth.

BABYLON - THE LION WITH WINGS OF AN EAGLE DANIEL 7:4

The first was like a lion and had the wings of an eagle. I kept looking until its wings were plucked, and it was lifted up from the ground and made to stand on two feet like a man; a human mind also was given to it.

The Lion of Babylon is an ancient Babylonian symbol. The Lion of Babylon symbolically represented the King of Babylon. This depiction is based on the Mesopotamian lion, which used to roam in the region. The wings being plucked is a reference to the time when God had humbled Nebuchadnezzar. God had caused Nebuchadnezzar to lose his mind and become like an animal for seven years. He was then restored and given back his kingdom after which he acknowledged the sovereignty of God. This is recorded in detail in Daniel Chapter 4.

THE BEAR (MEDO – PERSIA)

DANIEL 7:5

And behold, another beast, a second one, resembling a bear. And it was raised up on one side, and three ribs were in its mouth between its teeth; and thus, they said to it, 'Arise, devour much meat!'

The Bear represented the joint kingdom of the Medo - Persians. The Persians were more powerful than the Medes as represented by the raised side. Before the two kingdoms united, Media was the dominant kingdom. But in 550 B.C., the Medes came under the control of Persian King Cyrus II, who thereafter ruled over the kingdom of Medo-Persia. Centered in the region north of the Persian Gulf, this vast realm eventually stretched from the Aegean Sea to Egypt to northwestern India and included Judea.

Medo-Persia ruled over the Jewish nation for more than 200 years—from the overthrow of Babylon in 539 B.C. until Medo-Persia itself was defeated by the Greeks in 331 B.C.

THE LEOPARD (GREECE)

DANIEL 7:6

After this I kept looking, and behold, another one, like a leopard, which had on its back four wings of a bird; the beast also had four heads, and dominion was given to it.

The Grecian empire under the dynamic young leader Alexander the Great swept over this entire region. The Leopard is a strong and swift animal. The four wings represented the speed in which Alexander would conquer nation after nation. In a period of just ten years, he had an empire that stretched from Greece to the borders of India. Thereafter, Alexander continued to expand his empire until his premature death in 323 B.C., at the age of 32.

The four heads represent the division of the kingdom into four major parts after Alexander.

No single individual succeeded Alexander as absolute ruler, nor did any of his offspring. Rather, his four leading generals—Lysimachus, Cassander, Seleucus, and Ptolemy—"proclaimed themselves kings" and took over the empire.

THE TERRIBLE 4TH BEAST (ROME)

DANIEL 7:7

After this I kept looking in the night visions, and behold, a fourth beast, dreadful and terrifying and extremely strong; and it had large iron teeth. It devoured and crushed and trampled down the remainder with its feet; and it was different from all the beasts that were before it, and it had ten horns.

In 168 B.C., it was the Roman Empire's turn to enact its supreme rule upon the region.

Prophetically this terrible looking beast perfectly symbolizes this kingdom: its military strength and discipline, its domination over many conquered nations, its laws imposed on all people far and wide.

The Roman Empire was in power during the time of Jesus and continued to rule through its capital Rome till 324 A.D.

Constantinople became the new capital of the Roman Empire through Emperor Constantine the Great, after whom it was named, and dedicated on 11 May 330. The city was located in what are now the European side and the core of modern Istanbul. It is located in Turkey.

The Western part of Rome collapsed under the onslaught of the barbarian tribes.

The Eastern part of Rome continued as the Byzantine Empire until the year 1453 A.D. when it was taken over by the Ottoman Empire.

It is in this geographical area that comprises Turkey and the Middle-East going right up to India, parts of North Africa and a very small portion of Eastern Europe that the Bible draws our attention to. This area is completely dominated by Islam. What is important to note is that Islam is a political religion that demands complete dominance of the world.

THE TEN HORNS AND THE "LITTLE HORN"

The Ten horns represent ten kings who will arise just prior the second coming of Jesus.

But they will be led by an individual whom the Bible calls "The Little Horn"

This Man will oppose God and speak abominations against the "Son of God" – Jesus

DANIEL 7:24

As for the ten horns, out of this kingdom ten kings will arise;

THE "LITTLE HORN" DANIEL 7:24-25

and another will arise after them, and he will be different from the previous ones and will subdue three kings. He will speak out against the Highest and wear down the saints of the Highest One, and he will intend to make alterations in times and in law; and they will be given into his hand for a time, times, and half a time.

DANIEL 7:20-22

.... the other horn which came up, and before which three of them fell, namely, that horn which had eyes and a mouth uttering great boasts and which was larger in appearance than its associates. I kept looking, and that horn was waging war with the saints and overpowering them until the Ancient of Days came and judgment was passed in favor of the saints of the Highest One, and the time arrived when the saints took possession of the kingdom.

The Bible gives us a glimpse of the person who would be leading the "Ten kings" and calls him the "Little Horn. He will be different and unlike the kings before him. He will be a vile man who will not only oppose God but also severely persecute the people of God. He will attempt to make changes in the Law and institute unholy laws. The people of God will be given into his hand for a time called "*a time, times, and half a time.*" This is a period of three and a half years.

During the three and a half years the "Little Horn" whom many also refer to as "The Anti-Christ causes great distress to the people of God. But He is judged and taken away to be cast into the "Lake of fire"

THE STATUE OF NEBUCHADNEZZAR AND THE FOUR BEASTS.

Both point to the same four kingdoms. They are Babylon, Medo - Persia, Greece and Rome.

The ten toes of the statue are the same as the ten horns on the 4th beast.

The Ten Horns are ten kings who will arise in the last days to oppose the people of God and take control of the world.

A careful reading of the scripture seems to point to a unique situation

As we ponder on the dream of the Statute of Nebuchadnezzar, we must remember that the toes and the feet were a mixture of two kinds of seed; human and angelic. But the angels were of the "fallen" kind.

Jesus taught us about the conditions that will prevail in the last days. This will be the situation that will prevail just before His return. He gave us two examples. One is the example of Noah and the other is the example of Lot the nephew of Abraham.

What were the highlights of their social conditions before the flood?

The advent of fallen Angels inter- marrying with humans. The result was the birth of the Nephilim (The fallen Ones). We have only to open our eyes and see the literature and the kind of movies that are being produced these days. Supernatural humans are shown as super heroes who save humanity.

The highlight of the city of Sodom and Gomorrah where Lot lived was homosexuality. This life style is not only openly promoted but laws are being put into place to make it an offence to speak against it.

The spiritual atmosphere is being set for the end time battle for the souls of men.

COMPARISON CHART

DANIEL CHAPTER 2	DANIEL CHAPTER 7	NATION	
Head of Gold	Lion	Babylon	
Breast of Silver	Bear	Medo – Persia	

Waist of Bronze	Leopard	Greece	
Legs of Iron	Terrible Beast	Rome	
Feet of Iron and clay	Ten Horns	Ten kings	
	Little Horn		The "Anti-Christ"
The Rock that conquers	The "Son of Man"	The Kingdom of God	

THE SOVEREIGN GOD WILL RULE – DANIEL 7:26-27

But the court will sit for judgment, and his dominion will be taken away, annihilated and destroyed forever. Then the sovereignty, the dominion and the greatness of all the kingdoms under the whole heaven will be given to the people of the saints of the Highest One; His kingdom will be an everlasting kingdom, and all the dominions will serve and obey Him.'

Then the sovereignty, dominion and greatness of all the kingdoms under heaven will be given to the people of the saints of God. Jesus is the ruler of this kingdom that will reign forever. All nations and people of every language and tongue will serve and obey Him.

THE KINGDOM OF JESUS - DANIEL 7:9-14

I kept looking Until thrones were set up,
And the Ancient of Days took His seat;
His vesture was like white snow and the hair of His head like pure wool.
His throne was ablaze with flames; its wheels were a burning fire.
"A river of fire was flowing and coming out from before Him;
Thousands upon thousands were attending Him,
And myriads upon myriads were standing before Him;
The court sat,
And the books were opened.

Then I kept looking because of the sound of the boastful words which the horn was speaking; I kept looking until the beast was slain, and its body was destroyed and given to burning fire.

As for the rest of the beasts, their dominion was taken away, but an extension of life was granted to them for an appointed period of time.

Here we are given a spectacular glimpse of the way events will unfold in the future.

We are introduced to this diabolical person called the "little Horn" who not only blasphemes against the Living God but also tries to exalt himself with great boasting.

While all this is happening however, God is on the throne in Heaven. There is the scene of a courtroom where the books are opened. The "Little Horn" is judged and cast into the lake of fire.

JESUS – THE KING OF KINGS" – DANIEL 7:13-14

"I kept looking in the night visions,
And behold, with the clouds of heaven One like a Son of Man was coming,
And He came up to the Ancient of Days and was presented before Him.
"And to Him was given dominion, Glory and a kingdom,
That all the peoples, nations and men of every language might serve Him.
His dominion is an everlasting dominion which will not pass away;
And His kingdom is one which will not be destroyed.

The "Son of Man" is presented before the Father and is given dominion, glory and a kingdom.

It is a kingdom that will never pass away and all the peoples, nations and men of every language will serve Him. His kingdom will never be destroyed.

CHAPTER 3

ISRAEL FAILS TO RECOGNIZE THE MESSIAH

Daniel the prophet had gone into captivity along with the inhabitants of Jerusalem when Babylon had defeated them in 605 B.C. The Babylonian king Nebuchadnezzar had not only destroyed the city but also the central part of Jewish life which was the Jewish Temple.

Daniel had risen to the second highest position in Babylon. He was highly respected and when the Babylonians were defeated by the Medo – Persians, he continued to retain his position among the bureaucracy of the empire.

The Jewish people had been in captivity though out this time in Babylon. It was now almost 70 years since they were in exile. Daniel was a young man when he was taken captive. Now he was an old man. Daniel knew from the writings of Jeremiah the prophet, that God would give His people freedom and allow them to return to Jerusalem after a period of 70 years.

In the 1st year of the reign of Darius the Median king, Daniel turned to seek direction from the Lord. He sought the Lord with prayer and fasting. He wanted to know what would happen to his people and their holy city Jerusalem. God sent the Angel Gabriel in answer to Daniel's supplication.

A PERIOD OF "SEVENTY TIMES SEVEN"

God had ordained a period of seventy weeks or a period of 490 years to give the people of Israel another chance. But this time they would not only be restored into their land but also get back their Temple. This time they would get an opportunity to meet with their Messiah.

It was a time frame that God would give the Jewish people to repent, receive their Messiah and take their place as the favored people among the Nations of the Earth.

At stake was also the city of Jerusalem.

The Messiah would come at a specific time in history and would accomplish these things for his people.

DANIEL 9:24

"Seventy weeks have been decreed for your people and your holy city,

- *to finish the transgression,*
- *to make an end of sin,*
- *to make atonement for iniquity,*
- *to bring in everlasting righteousness,*
- *to seal up vision and prophecy and*
- *to anoint the most holy place.*

DANIEL 9:25

So you are to know and discern that from the issuing of a decree to restore and rebuild Jerusalem until Messiah the Prince there will be seven weeks and sixty-two weeks; it will be built again, with plaza and moat, even in times of distress.

In the passage, God told Daniel (through His angel)

1. That He was giving the Jews one last chance to repent of their sins,
2. To reconcile with God,
3. To prepare for their coming Messiah, who would arrive in the 70th week of the prophecy.

The "weeks" were not ordinary days at all, but sevens of years. Every day of these 70 weeks represented a prophetic year and we can prove it through historical events.

THE 490 YEARS WOULD BE BROKEN INTO THREE PARTS.

7 weeks or 49 years

62 weeks or 434 years

1 week or 7 years

From the issuing of the decree, to the coming of the Messiah there would be a period of "Seven weeks" and "Sixty-two weeks".

The Angel explained to Daniel that the city and its streets would be rebuilt, but in difficult times. The Jews would know the starting date from the decree that would announce the rebuilding of the city. If we scroll back through history, we find that there were four decrees that were announced by the Medo- Persian kings with relation to Jerusalem.

When would the date of the 490 years begin?

INITIATOR	PASSAGE	DATE	PARTICULARS OF THE DECREE
Cyrus	Ezra 1:1-4	539 B.C.	Allowed the Jews to return home and rebuild their Temple. The work ceased because of false allegations (Ezra 4:6-13).

Darius	Ezra 6:8-12	520 B.C.	Allowed the Jews to complete the rebuilding of the Temple
Artaxerxes	Ezra 7:11-26	457 B.C.	Gave authority to Ezra to lead the nation in the Laws of God.
Artaxerxes	Nehemiah 1	445 B.C.	Gave permission to Nehemiah to rebuild the walls of Jerusalem.

Ezra was given this mandate in the 7th year of Artaxerxes.

Allowing for his ascension year, this Persian king began his reign in 464 B.C.

This places the king's decree to Ezra around 457 B.C.

(464 B.C minus 7 years = 457 B.C.)

We find Ezra also alludes to possibly been given permission in his prayer not only to rebuild the Temple but also to build the walls of Judah and Jerusalem.

EZRA 9:9

"For we are slaves; yet in our bondage our God has not forsaken us, but has extended loving Kindness to us in the sight of the kings of Persia, to give us reviving to raise up the house of Our God, restore its ruins and to give us a wall in Judah and Jerusalem."

WHEN WAS THE MESSIAH REVEALED TO THE JEWS?

God was giving not only the timeline, but also the accomplishments that the Messiah would do for his people. If we follow the timeline, we come to the year 27 A.D. The very year John the Baptist began preaching in the wilderness. The very year John baptized Jesus and declared that Jesus was "the lamb that takes away the sins of the world"

DANIEL 9:25

So you are to know and discern that from the issuing of a decree to restore and rebuild Jerusalem until Messiah the Prince there will be seven weeks and sixty-two weeks;

LET'S DO SOME MATH

7 x 7 = 49 years

62 x 7 = 434 years

The total would be 483 years

The calculation should be **457 – 483 – 1 = 27 A.D.**

Remember not to count year zero going from B.C. to A.D. because this will produce a one-year error.

These 483 years gives us the time frame from the issuing of the Decree to rebuild Jerusalem, till the Messiah is presented to the people of Israel. This is the time when John the Baptist began his public ministry. He had pointed to Jesus as the Lamb of God who had come to take away the sins of the world.

Jesus had begun His public ministry at the age of 30.

HISTORICAL EVIDENCE.

Using the historical evidence of the starting date of 457 B.C. for the decree to rebuild Jerusalem and the fifteenth year of the reign of Tiberius Caesar, (Luke 3:1) while allowing for the one year of joint rule with Augustus, gives us the identical date of 27 A.D. verifying it is correct.

THE LAST WEEK

There remains however another period of "One Week" or a period of seven years.

What would happen in these last seven years?

Here is where it gets interesting.

A very popular opinion is that the last seven years are in the future. Accordingly, the last seven years are called the Tribulation period. Israel will make a covenant with the "Anti-Christ" for a period of seven years.

The "Anti-Christ" will allow the Jewish Temple to be built on the holy site. Sacrifices and offering would resume just like they were offered during the time of the first two Temples. In the middle of the seven years, the "Anti-Christ" will break his covenant with the people of Israel, and after declaring himself as God would persecute them.

According to this view, the church would be in heaven during this period of seven years.

But there is a difficulty with this view. The problem is that we have to assume that the seventy-week period is broken up. We do not have the mandate from the scriptures to take this liberty.

Let us take a couple of examples. When the Israelites were told that they would be in the wilderness for forty years, it was exactly forty years at a stretch. Similarly, when the Israelites were sent into captivity for seventy years into Babylon, it was in accordance with the warning given to Judah by the prophet Jeremiah.

In the same way when the Lord gave Israel a period of "Seventy weeks" it is to be taken in continuity.

DANIEL 9:26

Then after the sixty-two weeks the Messiah will be cut off and have nothing,

The Messiah was "cut off" points to the death of Jesus on the Cross. He will be put to death not for Himself, but for us all. His death was prophesied in detail in Isaiah 53. He will lay down His life as a sacrifice for the sins of mankind.

With His death and resurrection, the Messiah would accomplish these things for His people;

- to finish the transgression,
- to make an end of sin,
- to make atonement for iniquity,
- to bring in everlasting righteousness,
- to seal up vision and prophecy and
- to anoint the most holy place.

DANIEL 9:7

And he will make a firm covenant with the many for one week, but in the middle of the week he will put a stop to sacrifice and grain offering;

CRUCIFICATION DATE

So now we know that Jesus revealed Himself as the Messiah in 27 A.D.

This also gives us the crucifixion date of 31 A.D. with no complications in reconciling any of the dates with the historical and Biblical evidence. This was in the middle of the last seven years.

WHO MAKES A COVENANT WITH MANY PEOPLE

Is the one who makes the Covenant, the Messiah or the "Anti-Christ"?

ISAIAH 42:5-7

"I am the Lord; I have called You in righteousness,
I will also hold You by the hand and watch over You,
And I will appoint You as a covenant to the people,
As a light to the nations,
To open blind eyes,

To bring out prisoners from the dungeon
And those who dwell in darkness from the prison.

In this chapter of Isaiah 42, GOD is talking about His Son Jesus. Jesus is the one who will set the captives free. He is the one who will be appointed as a Covenant to the nations. The one who makes the Covenant is the Messiah and not the Anti-Christ.

WHO PUTS AN END TO THE SACRIFICE?

Jesus died and rose again. He became our High Priest who entered into heaven, not with the blood of goats and sheep but with His own blood.

Just as in the tabernacle and later in the temple, the High Priest would enter into the Most Holy place with the blood of animals and sprinkle the Mercy seat with the blood, so Jesus entered heaven and brought His own blood to the Mercy Seat.

The death of Jesus would also usher in a change in the manner in which the sacrifices for sins would be handled according to the Old Covenant. Now with the death of Jesus, He had ushered in the New Covenant which He established with His own blood. Now no longer would animals need to be sacrificed each year as a covering for the sins of the people.

Could a third Temple be built in Jerusalem in the last days?

There are clear indications that the Anti-Christ will declare himself as God and demand worship from all mankind. Jerusalem will be the epicenter during the rule of the Anti-Christ.

WHAT HAPPENS AT THE END OF THE SEVENTH WEEK?

The remaining 3.5 literal years brings us to the end of the 70 weeks and the Jewish probation.

The disciples labored mainly among the Jews during those three and a half years.

In 34 A.D., the 70 weeks ended when the Jews rejected the Gospel and stoned Stephen. The Jews had rejected the Gospel message and so the Gospel began to go to the Gentiles. (Acts 8:4). The Jews now receive salvation as individuals in the same the Gentiles do.

At the end of the last week, Jesus made a Covenant not only between Himself and the Jewish nation, but with the people of all nations. Any individual who has repented and received Him as their Messiah can now receive forgiveness for their sins.

No longer would men and women have to come to God with grain offerings and the blood sacrifices. The only acceptable sacrifice for the forgiveness of sins was accomplished by Jesus when He dies on the cross to save us.

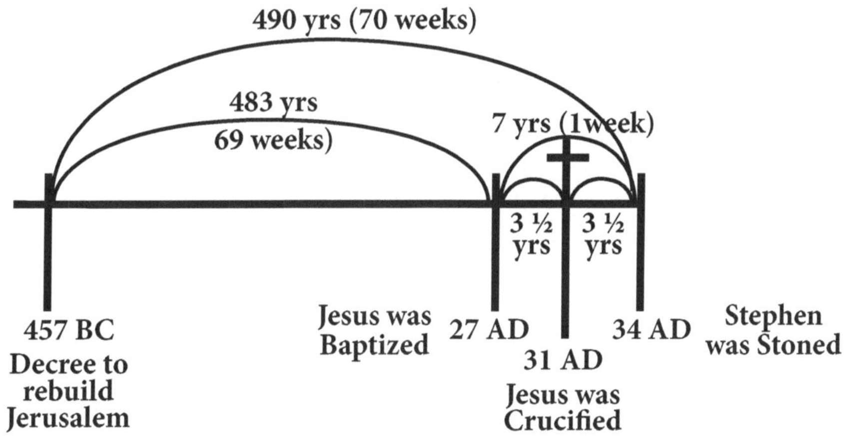

THE COST OF REJECTING THE MESSIAH

The Jewish nation has rejected their Messiah. The One whom they were looking forward to for generations, had come in their midst and yet they did not recognize Him. In fact, the Jewish leadership had accused Him of blasphemy and sent Him to be hung on a Cross.

The Jews had been expecting a Messiah who would come in great power, defeat all their enemies and raise the nation of Israel as the center of the world.

They had known from the writings of the Prophet Isaiah that the Messiah would rule from Zion over the nations of the world. Jerusalem would be at the Centre of all world events.

What they had missed out was that the Prophet Isaiah had also written that the Messiah would suffer and give His life as ransom for the sins of the people.

When Jesus did great miracles and performed great signs and wonders among the people, the Jewish authorities accused Him of getting His power not from God but from the Evil One.

Jesus Himself had warned them that as they had rejected Him, the nation would pay a heavy price. When He looked upon the city of Jerusalem in the last few days before He was crucified, Jesus wept over the city.

MATTHEW 23:37-38

"Jerusalem, Jerusalem, who kills the prophets and stones those who are sent to her!

How often I wanted to gather your children together, the way a hen gathers her chicks under her wings, and you were unwilling. Behold, your house is being left to you desolate!

Jesus warned that the city of Jerusalem would be left desolate. Not only would the city be destroyed, but also the Temple so that not one stone would be left upon another.

DANIEL 9:26

.....and the people of the prince who is to come will destroy the city and the sanctuary. And its end will come with a flood; even to the end there will be war; desolations are determined.

DANIEL 9:27

.......and on the wing of abominations will come one who makes desolate, even until a complete destruction, one that is decreed, is poured out on the one who makes desolate."

The people of the prince who would make the city and the Sanctuary desolate were the Romans and the prince who would lead them was Titus the son of the Roman Emperor Vespasian.

- This historical fact happened during the destruction of Jerusalem in 70 A.D.
- Over a million Jews were killed and hundreds of thousands were sold as slaves.
- The Jews were scattered among the nations.
- The city was now left desolate.

The city of Jerusalem and the nation of Israel continued to remain in desolation until in the beginning of the 20th Century, when the Jews began to return to the Promised Land.

The land of Israel has revived as the Jews have returned to their land of promise. God had promised His people through the Prophet Ezekiel that before the last days, the people would live in their land once again.

The Jewish people have been in constant danger from their enemies who surround them. A time is coming in the near future when once again they will be severely tested and face great trouble.

But this time the Messiah will come to their rescue. Not as the "Lamb of God" but as "the lion Of Judah."

CHAPTER 4

JESUS SUMMARIZES THE LAST DAYS

The disciples were in awe of the Jewish temple as its beauty was breath taking. It truly was a very beautiful and an awesome sight to behold. This in fact was the second Temple which King Herod had spared no expense in beautifying. It was the centre of religious, political and social life for the people of Israel.

But Jesus had just told them that the temple would be destroyed. The disciples were perplexed. They had some questions.

In fact, two specific questions:

MATTHEW 24: 1-3

Jesus came out from the temple and was going away when His disciples came up to point out the temple buildings to Him. And He said to them, "Do you not see all these things? Truly I say to you, not one stone here will be left upon another, which will not be torn down."

As He was sitting on the Mount of Olives, the disciples came to Him privately, saying, "Tell us, when will these things happen, and what will be the sign of Your coming, and of the end of the age?"

1. When will the Temple be destroyed?
2. When will Jesus' return and what will be the signs that His return is near?

Jesus began to explain to them the course of events that would unfold from then on to the end of the age. He began by identifying the signs that the disciples need to be alert about.

SIGNS IN THE WORLD

1. Wars and kingdoms against kingdoms	Matthew 24:6-7
2. Famines and earthquakes	Matthew 13:8
3. Plagues	Luke 21:11

SIGNS IN THE CHURCH

1. Deception
2. Persecution
3. A falling away and betrayal
4. False prophets will mislead many
5. The love of many will go cold due to lawlessness
6. The Gospel will be preached to the Nations

All these signs have been happening with increasing intensity as the coming of Jesus draws near. Remember Jesus said that these signs would be like the birth pangs that a woman in labor experiences. As the birth of the child draws near, the birth pangs will intensify.

Although it is not easy to get a time- line from these signs, we do have the nation of Israel as a prophetic time clock by which we can know the season we live in.

WHEN WOULD THE TEMPLE BE DESTROYED?

LUKE 21:5-7

And while some were talking about the temple, that it was adorned with beautiful stones and votive gifts, He said, "As for these things which you are looking at, the days will come in which there will not be left one stone upon another which will not be torn down."

They questioned Him, saying, "Teacher, when therefore will these things happen? And what will be the sign when these things are about to take place?"

THE EVENTS THAT WILL FOLLOW FOR ISRAEL AND THE TEMPLE – LUKE 21:20-24

"But when you see Jerusalem surrounded by armies, then recognize that her desolation is near. Then those who are in Judea must flee to the mountains, and those who are in the midst of the city must leave, and those who are in the country must not enter the city; because these are days of vengeance, so that all things which are written will be fulfilled. Woe to those who are pregnant and to those who are nursing babies in those days; for there will be great distress upon the land and wrath to this people; and they will fall by the edge of the sword, and will be led captive into all the nations; and Jerusalem will be trampled underfoot by the Gentiles until the times of the Gentiles are fulfilled.

With their rejection of the Messiah, Jesus had rightly predicted that Jerusalem and the nation of Israel would be left desolate. Jesus also warned that the Temple would be torn down and not one stone would be left upon another.

In 70 A.D., the Romans under the general Titus besieged the city of Jerusalem and a prolonged battle began for the city of Jerusalem. Over a million Jews were killed and over a million Jews were sold as slaves. The temple was torn down and not one stone remained upon another. Jerusalem was left desolate.

Jerusalem has been trampled underfoot by Gentile nations for almost 1900 years. This was the "Times of the Gentiles". In 1948 the Jews got back their nation after miraculously defeating the Arab Nations who tried to destroy them.

The place where the Temple had been constructed however remained in enemy hands until the war of 1967 when the Israel army defeated the Arab Nations that sought once again to destroy them.

The Bible mentions two "Times".

One is "The Time of the Gentiles" and the "Time of the End".

The Time of the Gentiles ended in 1967 when Jerusalem came under Israel rule after a gap of 2000 years. We are now at the period of time which the Bible calls "The Time of the End."

WHAT CAN WE EXPECT IN THE NEAR FUTURE FOR ISRAEL ?

The nation of Israel is a marvel among the nations of the world today. It has beaten the odds and survived as a nation under extremely trying conditions. The Jews experienced the dark days of the Holocaust in Germany where around 6 million Jews were massacred under Hitler. The Jews survived the "Pogroms" to destroy them in the Soviet Union and in Poland.

They were hounded and targeted in many nations. The Jewish outcry for a nation of their own grew more and more desperate. They understood that they needed to be back in the land promised to them by God which their forefathers had possessed for thousands of years.

Slowly but surely in small and large groups they came. Today there are over seven million Jews who have returned to the Promised Land. And the number keeps increasing.

Today although surrounded on all sides by Islamic nations who have vowed to annihilate them, they have thrived. They do not own any oil resources and have had to depend on ingenuity and innovation to succeed.

And succeed they did and how!! They are among the world leaders in innovation and technology. They not only export high tech equipment and other goods but are also a nation that exports a large amount of fruit and vegetables to the world. It is not surprising as God promised to bless them when He brought them back to their land.

It has the most powerful army in the Middle East and now has a peace treaty with Egypt and increasing ties with the rest of the world nations.

But the Bible warns that it is precisely at a time like this that a time of severe testing will come upon the nation.

ZECHARIAH 14:1-2

Behold, a day is coming for the LORD when the spoil taken from you will be divided among you.

For I will gather all the nations against Jerusalem to battle, and the city will be captured, the houses plundered, the women ravished and half of the city exiled, but the rest of the people will not be cut off from the city.

The nation of Israel would experience such trouble that their very survival would be at stake. Jesus describes this time of trouble will be unlike any nation has faced before or will face later. The nations of the Earth will be gathered against it to destroy it. The city will be captured, houses plundered, women raped and half the city will be exiled. The people will flee to try and get to safety elsewhere. But the rest of the people will still fight for their city and nation.

There will be such an urgency, that Jesus He tells the people to pray that they would not have to flee during the Sabbath day or in the winter. Nursing mothers and those pregnant would be severely under pressure.

Jesus had warned that just prior to His coming, the Jewish Nation will be tested like never before. Unless God cuts short this testing, none of the elect would survive.

But when should they flee the city?

Jesus now points to a prophecy given by Daniel the Prophet.

MATTHEW 24:15-22

"Therefore, when you see the ABOMINATION OF DESOLATION which was spoken of through Daniel the prophet, standing in the holy place (let the reader understand), then those who are in Judea must flee to the mountains. Whoever is on the housetop must not go down to get the things out that are in his house. Whoever is in the field must not turn back to get his cloak. But woe to those who are pregnant and to those who are nursing babies in those days!

But pray that your flight will not be in the winter, or on a Sabbath. For then there will be a great tribulation, such as has not occurred since the beginning of the world until now, nor ever will. Unless those days had been cut short, no life would have been saved; but for the sake of the elect those days will be cut short.

WHAT PROPHECY OF DANIEL IS JESUS POINTING TO?

In the 12th chapter of Daniel, the prophet wrote about the "End Times".

It will be a time of great testing for the people of Israel. It will be a time of refining, purging and preparing for the coming of their Messiah.

But this time of great trouble will come from another man who claims to be the Messiah.

The book of Daniel calls this man of evil as "The Little Horn".

The New Testament refers to him as the "Man of Sin"

He is often referred by the apostle John as "The Anti –Christ"

DANIEL 12:1-3

"Now at that time Michael, the great prince who stands guard over the sons of your people, will arise. And there will be a time of distress such as never occurred since there was a nation until that time; and at that time your people, everyone who is found written in the book, will be rescued.

Many of those who sleep in the dust of the ground will awake, these to everlasting life, but the others to disgrace and everlasting contempt. Those who have insight will shine brightly like the brightness of the expanse of heaven, and those who lead the many to righteousness, like the stars forever and ever.

All these events will happen just before the "second coming of the Messiah." Daniel was told that this time of trouble that would come upon his nation would precede the day of resurrection of the righteous. Just as the scriptures in the New Testament point to the resurrection of the saints who received Jesus as their Messiah, even those who are alive in Jesus will be caught up with Him to meet Him in the clouds.

When Daniel asks the angel about the time that this resurrection would take place, he is given a sign that the people of God should look for.

DANIEL 12:7

.......it would be for a time, times, and half a time; and as soon as they finish shattering the power of the holy people, all these events will be completed.

Daniel is told by the Angel that the people of God would face a very severe trial for three and a half years and their power would be shattered. But what event will convince the people of Israel to flee from Judah? It is a situation which Jesus refers to as the "Abomination that causes Desolation"

Daniel the prophet gives a time frame for this Abomination.

DANIEL 12:11-12

From the time that the regular sacrifice is abolished and the abomination of desolation is set up, there will be 1,290 days. How blessed is he who keeps waiting and attains to the 1,335 days!

HOW SHOULD WE INTERPRET THIS?

First let's see what the "Abomination that causes desolation" means. In the 11th chapter of Daniel, we are given a real-life situation that happened in the history of the nation of Israel. Israel had disobeyed the commands of God and had neglected the warning of the prophets to repent. This happened over a period of hundreds of years.

The northern part of the nation of Israel was first sent into captivity by the Assyrian kingdom. The 10 tribes which comprised the northern kingdom were then scattered into other parts of the world. The Southern kingdom of Judah was taken into captivity by the Babylonians.

Although they returned to their land, they continued to be ruled by the Medo- Persians, the Greeks and then the Romans.

When they were under Grecian rule, the kingdom of Greece broke up into four major parts. The north east part of the kingdom came under the rule of the Seleucid dynasty. A king arose at that time named Antiochus Epiphanies. He conquered Israel and tried to bring in Grecian influence in Judah. When he was opposed, he entered the Jewish Temple and slaughtered a pig on the altar to worship the Greek God Zeus. This happened in 167 B.C.

He ordered his soldiers to cut down without mercy those whom they met and to slay those who took refuge in their houses. There was a massacre of young and old, a killing of women and children, a slaughter of virgins and infants. In the space of three days, eighty thousand were lost, forty thousand meeting a violent death, and the same number being sold into slavery.

Jesus warned that something similar would happen at the time of the great trouble that the people of Israel would face. Through the book of Daniel as well as the book of Revelation, the Bible points to a person who would come not only to oppose and blaspheme God, but would persecute the people of God.

THE TIME THAT THE "ABOMINATION WOULD BE SET UP"

Here the prophet Daniel points to a time when the regular sacrifices are abolished. Since this Abomination is to be at the cost of the regular sacrifice, many scholars believe that the Jewish Temple will have to be built once again for the sacrifices to be held. It is believed that at some time the "Anti-Christ will stop the sacrifices and declare himself to be God at the Temple.

There is however a major problem for the Temple to be rebuilt. At this very moment there exists on the very spot an Islamic Mosque called Al -Aqsa. This mosque is considered the 3rd holiest site for the Muslims.

From the time of the abolition to the setting up of the "Abomination that causes desolation" the time given is 1290 days. Taking in consideration that the Jewish month consists of 30 days, this would mean a time of three years and seven months. Could this be a time after the period of three and half years that the bible announces as the terrible trouble that will come upon the nation?

A DAY FOR A YEAR THEORY

Some scholars believe that the three and a half years or the 1260 days is actually a period of 1260 years. In that case we then have to look back before the book of Daniel. The Babylonians destroyed the first Jewish Temple in the year 586 B.C. But sacrifices continued at the place as mentioned in the book of Jeremiah until the year 583 B.C.

Suppose we take "the day as a year" principle and add 1290 years. Taking into account that the Jewish year consists of 360 days instead of the 365 days, we now have 1271 years.

This brings us to the year 688 A.D.

So why is this year significant? In the year 688 A.D. the Caliph Abd El Malik ibn Marwan began the construction of what is now called the "The Dome of the Rock". This was a monument to mark the exact spot which the Muslims believe that Mohammad went up to heaven.

Some scholars believe that the 'Dome of the Rock" is the Abomination that the prophet is talking about. The "man of Sin" or the "Anti-Christ will begin his rule from this place declaring himself to be God.

Jesus specifically warned that at this time there would be those who claim to be Jesus the Messiah. He had also warned about false prophets who would do such miracles so as to deceive even the elect if were possible.

But the coming of Jesus would be very visible for all to see.

CHAPTER 5

THE OLIVET DISCOURSE AND THE BOOK OF REVELATION

The Olivet discourse is a prophetic presentation given to us by the Lord regarding the future of the Church as well as the nation of Israel. Looking back at the history of the last 2000 years, we have very clear proof that God has given us a blueprint in His word, of the things that have already happened, as well as the things to come.

The Olivet discourse is recorded in three chapters of the Gospels.

1. Matthew 24
2. Mark 13
3. Luke 21

Through a careful study of these chapters, we get a vivid outline of how the future would pan out. Jesus gave the disciples a broad framework which we can look at and get the bigger picture. As the days for His return have come nearer the picture gets clearer.

THE SIGNS ON THE EARTH

1. Wars and nations rising against nations
2. Famines and earthquakes
3. Pestilences and death
4. Terror and great signs in the sky.

THE SIGNS IN THE CHURCH

1. Deception
2. Persecution
3. A falling away and betrayal
4. False prophets will mislead many
5. The love of many will go cold due to lawlessness
6. The Gospel will be preached to the Nations

These signs were birth pangs which would intensify as the time for the Lord's return draws closer.

SIGNS SPECIFIC TO THE TIME OF THE EARLY CHURCH

LUKE 21:12-19

The disciples would face severe persecution. They would be delivered to the synagogues and prisons. They would be brought before kings and governors for the sake of Jesus name.

This would lead to an opportunity to testify about Jesus. They would be betrayed even by their own parents and relatives and some of them would be put to death. They would be hated by all because of the name of Jesus. Yet Jesus encouraged them that that even a hair of their head would not perish but in losing their lives they would gain it.

THE PROPHECY REGARDING THE NATION OF ISRAEL AND THE TEMPLE. – LUKE 21:20-24

Jesus had warned the disciples that in the near future, a day would come when Jerusalem would be surrounded by armies who would destroy Jerusalem and make it desolate. He had warned the disciples that as Jerusalem was being surrounded, they were to flee the city.

It would be a time of horror especially for those pregnant and those nursing babies. He warned of a time of great distress that would come upon the city and the people. They would fall by the edge of the sword, and would be led captive into all the nations of the world.

The city of Jerusalem would be trampled underfoot by the Gentiles until the "time of the Gentiles" was fulfilled. The Jewish Temple would be destroyed in such a way, that not one stone would be left upon the other. Not surprisingly everything happened just as Jesus had prophesied.

The Romans surrounded Jerusalem in the year 70 A.D. and not only destroyed the Temple but massacred the Jews. Over a million of them were killed and over a million were sold as slaves. Eventually they were banned from entering Jerusalem in 135 A.D and the region of Israel was renamed as Palestina.

The Jewish population dispersed into the nations of the world. They prospered in every nation they went into but also faced severe persecution and were hounded out of most nations they settled in. It took a horror like the Holocaust in Germany in which six million Jews were annihilated that made them desperate to come back to their land of promise after almost 2000 years.

They came back as a Nation in 1948 A.D., but it was only in the year 1967 A.D. that Jerusalem came under Jewish control. They have now resettled in the land in the millions.

The Nation has flourished despite unimaginable odds and the people now thrive in the land.

FUTURE SHOCK:

The prophet Ezekiel had predicted that God had planned to bring His people back to the Land.

This is recorded in Ezekiel Chapters 36 and 37. He would gather them from the nations in which they had been scattered and bring them back to Israel.

The land would once again flourish and the nations of the world would acknowledge the extraordinary turn of events in the rebirth of the nation. Though this would seem impossible, yet God would orchestrate world events so that the plan for His people would come to pass.

But the prophet Ezekiel also prophesied that when they had resettled in the land and were prosperous, they would continue to face grave danger from their surrounding enemies.

This would eventually culminate into a world- wide attempt from the armies of the world to destroy the Jewish people once and for all.

Jesus had also warned about a time of such tribulation that will come once again upon the nation of Israel that it has never happened before nor will happen again. The Prophet Zechariah had prophesied about a time that the people of Israel would be severely tested. This is recorded in the book of Zechariah.

ZECHARIAH 14:1-2

Behold, a day is coming for the LORD when the spoil taken from you will be divided among you. For I will gather all the nations against Jerusalem to battle, and the city will be captured, the houses plundered, the women ravished and half of the city exiled, but the rest of the people will not be cut off from the city.

The Book of Daniel (Chapter 12) also records this time of testing that will come upon all of God's elect. The people of the nation of Israel will be tested, purged and purified.

This time will last for a period of three and a half years.

This period is known as the "Great Tribulation."

During this time the people of God will be given into the hand of a person the Bible calls "The Little Horn". His other names include "The Man of Sin", The Anti-Christ" and "The Beast from the Sea"

DANIEL 12:1

"And there will be a time of distress such as never occurred since there was a nation until that time; and at that time your people, everyone who is found written in the book, will be rescued."

THE ABOMINATION THAT CAUSES DESOLATION"

Jesus describes an event called "The abomination that causes Desolation" which will occur at this time. In Mark Chapter 13:14-21 the Lord reminds His people that they are to watch out for this sign. Jesus also warns of false Messiah's and false Prophets who will arise and do such signs and wonders to deceive even the elect if possible.

The "Man of Sin" or "The Beast" will declare himself as God in Jerusalem and demand worship from everyone on the earth. He will blaspheme the true God and persecute the people of God. He will be assisted by the "False Prophet" who will do great signs and wonders so as to astonish the people of the Earth. Anyone who does not worship the Beast will be severely persecuted.

Satan will give his power and authority to this individual who embodies in person all that is evil. This will be a time of great Tribulation.

JESUS WARNED US NOT TO BE MISLED

Jesus warned the disciples that if anyone told them that Christ had come back in person once again, they were not to believe them. False Christ's and false prophets would arise and show great signs and wonders to mislead many.

The coming of Jesus would be evident to the entire world. Just as lightning flashes from the east as well as the west, so would His coming be very much in the open. The first time Jesus came to redeem mankind and to offer his life a ransom, so that all who believed in Him could be saved. His coming as a little child born in a little inn in Bethlehem was without much display of power. Only a select few knew about His coming.

But now He will come with great power and glory. His first coming was in the form of the "Lamb of God" who came to take away the sins of the world. Now he will come as "The Lion of Judah" and the "King of Kings" to execute God's wrath upon the world and its people who had corrupted the earth with evil.

SIGNS IN THE SKY - MATTHEW 24:29-30

"But immediately after the tribulation of those days THE SUN WILL BE DARKENED, AND THE MOON WILL NOT GIVE ITS LIGHT, AND THE STARS WILL FALL from the sky, and the powers of the heavens will be shaken. And then the sign of the Son of Man will appear in the sky, and then all the tribes of the earth will mourn, and they will see the SON OF MAN COMING ON THE CLOUDS OF THE SKY with power and great glory.

THE ELECT ARE GATHERED AT THE LAST TRUMPET -MATTHEW 24:31

And He will send forth His angels with A GREAT TRUMPET and THEY WILL GATHER TOGETHER His elect from the four winds, from one end of the sky to the other.

THE SIGNS THAT JESUS GAVE US AS A WARNING

1. Deceptions

2. Wars and Nations fighting against Nations.
3. Famines and earthquakes
4. Pestilences and death
5. Persecution of God's people and martyrdom.
6. The signs in the sky declaring the return of Jesus.
7. The last trumpet and gathering of the Elect.

In between these signs, Jesus had given the disciples the events that would be woven in through history.

1. The disciples would be persecuted and many put to death for their faith.
2. The Church would be severely tested and many would fall away.
3. The Gospel would be preached to all nations.
4. Jerusalem would be surrounded and destroyed by invading armies in 70 A.D.
5. The temple would be destroyed.
6. Jerusalem would be trampled by Gentile nations until the Jewish nation would repossess it.
7. A severe time of testing would come upon the Jewish nation just prior to the coming of Jesus to save them.
8. This time of testing would be highlighted by an event called "The abomination of Desolation".

But in what way are these passages of scripture connected to the book of Revelation?

The book of revelation is also a prophetic guide to how the history of mankind will play out. When John the apostle was writing this book as an exile on the island of Patmos, he wrote down whatever was revealed to him by the angel sent by Jesus. He would not have fully understood what he was penning down under the inspiration of the Holy Spirit.

As we look back in history, we find that the Church has also tried to understand the revelation given to John. It does seem like a puzzle at times. But as the days of the coming of Jesus draws near, the revelation becomes clearer.

Our generation has the privilege of seeing the people of Israel back in their promised land. We can look back at history and look forward to prophecy through the lens of the Nation of Israel.

Even the Prophet Daniel was told by the Lord that the prophecy of the "End Times" was sealed until the "Times of the End."

Most Bible scholars believe that we are at that period in human history called "The End Times"

CONNECTING "THE BOOK OF REVELATION" TO THE "OLIVET DISCOURSE"

In the book of Revelation in Chapter 4, John is shown heaven and God the Father seated on His throne. He is surrounded by the four Living creatures, the twenty-four Elders and multitudes of angels. They are seen worshipping the Lord who is seated in splendor and majesty before a sea of glass which looks like crystal.

In His right-hand God has a scroll with seven Seals on it.

No one was found worthy to open the seals and read its contents. Inside the scroll is the revelation of the things that are to happen on the Earth.

We are then introduced to Jesus "The Lamb of God" who is also the "Lion of Judah".

He has overcome and is worthy to open the scroll after opening the Seven Seals.

The Seals are opened by Jesus. With the opening of each Seal, events that are to take place upon the earth are revealed. The introduction to the opening of the Seals is in the 6th Chapter of the book of Revelation.

THE FIRST SEAL—FALSE CHRISTS (REVELATION 6:1-2)

Then I saw when the Lamb broke one of the seven seals, and I heard one of the four living creatures saying as with a voice of thunder, "Come" I looked, and behold, a white horse, and he who sat on it had a bow; and a crown was given to him, and he went out conquering and to conquer.

THE SECOND SEAL—WAR (REVELATION 6:3-4)

When He broke the second seal, I heard the second living creature saying,

"Come." And another, a red horse, went out; and to him who sat on it, it was granted to take peace from the earth, and that men would slay one another; and a great sword was given to him.

THE THIRD SEAL—FAMINE (REVELATION 6:5-6)

When He broke the third seal, I heard the third living creature saying, "Come." I looked, and behold, a black horse; and he who sat on it had a pair of scales in his hand. And I heard something like a voice in the center of the four living creatures saying, "A quart of wheat for a denarius, and three quarts of barley for a denarius; and do not damage the oil and the wine."

THE FOURTH SEAL—DEATH (REVELATION 6:7-8)

When the Lamb broke the fourth seal, I heard the voice of the fourth living creature saying, "Come." I looked, and behold, an ashen horse; and he who sat on it had the name Death; and Hades was following with him. Authority was given to them over a fourth of the earth, to kill with sword and with famine and with pestilence and by the wild beasts of the earth.

THE FIFTH SEAL—MARTYRS (REVELATION 6:9-11)

When the Lamb broke the fifth seal, I saw underneath the altar the souls of those who had been slain because of the word of God, and because of the testimony which they had maintained; and they cried out with a loud voice, saying, "How long, O Lord, holy and true, will You refrain from judging and avenging our blood on those who dwell on the earth?"

And there was given to each of them a white robe; and they were told that they should rest for a little while longer, until the number of their fellow servants and their brethren who were to be killed even as they had been would be completed also.

THE SIXTH SEAL—SIGNS IN THE SKY (REVELATION 12-14)

I looked when He broke the sixth seal, and there was a great earthquake; and the sun became black as sackcloth made of hair, and the whole moon became like blood; and the stars of the sky fell to the earth, as a fig tree casts its unripe figs when shaken by a great wind.

The sky was split apart like a scroll when it is rolled up, and every mountain and island were moved out of their places.

GROUP OF SIGNS

	MATTHEW	LUKE	REVELATION
False Christs	24:4-5	21:4	6:1-2
Wars	24:6	21:9,10	6:3-4
Famines	24:7	21:11	6:5-6
Pestilence & Death	24:7-8	21:12	6:7-8
Martyrs	24:9	21:24	6:9-11
Signs in the sky	24:10-13	21:25	6:12-17

THE LAST TRUMPET - THE PEOPLE OF GOD CAUGHT UP IN THE CLOUDS TO MEET JESUS

There has been much discussion and debate about the time of the rapture. It is important to take account of the reality that the last trumpet and the Lord's return is after the time of tribulation.

A careful reading of the scripture's points to this event at the time of Jesus return.

Many have interpreted the passages of scripture in Revelation chapter 7:9-17 as the proof that the church will be in heaven while the rest of the world undergoes the time of testing that will come upon the world. But if we read the account of the sixth Seal, we find that when the world powers are shaken up, and the signs in the sky take place, it points to the entry of Jesus to take over the reins of the Earth forever.

THE SIXTH SEAL—SIGNS IN THE SKY (REVELATION 12-14)

I looked when He broke the sixth seal, and there was a great earthquake; and the sun became black as sackcloth made of hair, and the whole moon became like blood; and the stars of the sky fell to the earth, as a fig tree casts its unripe figs when shaken by a great wind. The sky was split apart like a scroll when it is rolled up, and every mountain and island were moved out of their places.

These passages reveal that apart from the signs with the sun and the moon, the stars of the sky fall to the earth. The sky is split apart like a scroll when it is rolled up. Every mountain and islands are moved out of their place. If every island and mountains are moved out of their place it pretty much means that it is the end of the "age of Man".

Now Jesus the Messiah who is the King of Kings will come and reign.

How then can we then explain the sequence of events that take place in the book of Revelation?

We have to contend with the sequence of the not only the 7 seals but also the 7 Trumpets and the 7 Bowls of wrath.

1ST OPINION

Some are of the opinion that they are sequential and happen in the order they are revealed.

The 7 Seals come first.

After that the church is taken up to heaven in Chapter 7.

Then the 7 Trumpets are blown which bring about great tribulation on the Earth as well as the wrath of God is poured out. This teaching advocates that the people who have not been saved will go through this time of trouble whereas the saved believers will be in heaven.

Then come the "Bowls" of wrath which are poured out by God upon the earth.

2ND OPINION

The other possibility that is proposed is that sequence of the Seals, the Trumpets and the Bowls are parallel events. The opening of the Seals is a summary of the entire turn out of events.

The Trumpets and Bowl judgments are the descriptions of what the opening of the Seals point towards.

THERE ARE THREE WAYS TO SEE THIS

i. They are successive.

ii. They are simultaneous.

iii. They are successive & simultaneous.

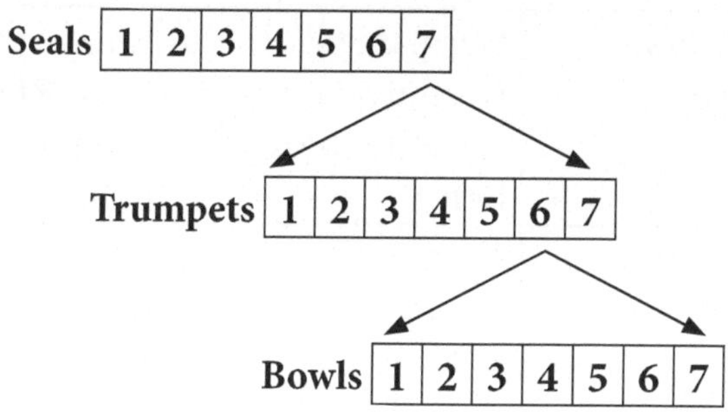

- The seventh seal, trumpet and bowls have a common feature and events.
- The combination is however more accurate. It's a combination of the two that seems to be a better fit.
- The six TRUMPETS are simultaneous to the six SEALS and six BOWLS are simultaneous to the six trumpets.
- The seventh of each of the seal, trumpet and bowl is the same event.

The order in which these things will happen is unclear but what is important to understand is that these things will happen and we must be ready.

THE SEALS, TRUMPETS AND BOWLS OF REVELATION			
NOS.	SEAL	TRUMPETS	BOWLS
I	White Horse - (Deception)	Hail, fire, blood 1/3 earth, trees, grass burned	Angel poured bowl on the ***EARTH*** Sores on people who had the Mark of the Beast and who worshipped his image
II	Red Horse - (War)	Mountain with fire thrown into sea,	Angel poured bowl into the ***SEA*** Every living creature died

III	Black Horse - (Famine)	Star named wormwood 1/3 water became bitter,	Angel poured into ***RIVERS*** and ***STREAMS*** They became blood
IV	Asher Horse - (Pestilence)	1/3 Sun, moon, stars were struck 1/3 became darkened	Angel poured bowl upon the ***SUN*** It scorched men with fierce heat
V	Martyrs --(Persecution)	Star from heaven fallen to earth Opened bottomless pit Locusts and Scorpions Torment for 5 months	Angel poured bowl on the ***THRONE OF THE BEAST.*** Kingdom became darkened. Gnawed their tongues because of sores and pain, but did not repent
VI	1) Earthquake 2) Sun/Moon 3) Sky, Figs 4) Men hide in terror	Release the 4 angels who are bound at Euphrates. 1/3 of mankind killed Armies of horsemen - 200 million 1/3 killed by fire, smoke, brimstone	Angel poured bowl on the ***RIVER OF EUPHARATES*** Water dried up Way prepared for the kings of the east
VII	Ushered in the Trumpets	Kingdoms of world have become kingdom of our Lord and Christ. The nations enraged - Your wrath has come. Time of judgment	Angel poured bowl upon the ***AIR*** Flashes of lightning and thunder. Earthquakes, cities of nation fell. Every island fled; mountains not found

Where do we place the passages of scripture in Revelation Chapter 7 that describes the people before the throne of God?

A careful reading of these passages and a comparison of Revelation chapter 22, we find a number of common descriptions.

	Revelation 7	Revelation 21 & 22
1. God's people before the Throne of God	v:9	Rev 22:4
2. God dwells with His people	v:15	Rev 21:3
3. The absence of the Sun and moon	v:16	Rev 22:5
4. God will wipe away the tears of his people	v:17	Rev 21:4

These passages describe the same situation. It is that time that when God dwells with Man.

Where does the event of the 1, 44,000 men of the twelve tribes of Israel fit?

This fits in to the time period of the 1000-year Millennium rule of Jesus on the earth.

In a nutshell, the future will pan out in this manner.

1st seal	-	Deceptions
2nd Seal	-	Wars
3rd Seal	-	Famines and earthquakes
4th Seal	-	Pestilences and Death
5th Seal	-	Persecution and Martyrs
		◆ All these Signs have been happening parallel for the last 2000 years
		◆ These Signs will accelerate as the coming of Jesus draws near.

		◆ The Trumpets and Bowl judgments are in line with the Seals
6th Seal	-	The Signs in the sky (The Sun Moon and stars)
		The people of God are caught up in the clouds to meet Jesus
		Jesus comes again to judge mankind
		The 1000-year rule of Jesus on the Earth
		The white throne Judgment
		The New Jerusalem

CHAPTER 6

THE UNHOLY ALLIANCE

The coalition of the "Beasts of Revelation"

The book of Revelation introduces us to a number of characters which are a mystery at a first glance. As we probe further, the identity of these characters becomes clearer, but our investigation does leave room for surprises.

In this topic we will try and get an understanding of three characters.

1. The Dragon
2. The Beast from the Sea
3. The Beast from the Earth.

A. THE DRAGON

Identifying this character is a bit easier as there are sufficient clues the Bible offers us.

In order to get the full picture though, we have to also identify the two signs that are given to us in Revelation Chapter 12.

THE FIRST SIGN IS OF A WOMAN. - REVELATION 12:1-2

A great sign appeared in heaven: a woman clothed with the sun, and the moon under her feet, and on her head a crown of twelve stars; and she was with child; and she cried out, being in labor and in pain to give birth.

The Bible gives us more information about this woman. She gives birth to a male child who will rule over the nations. At the time of the birth of the child, the Dragon attempts to kill the child. The child is later taken up to heaven where he is at the throne of God.

The woman is persecuted by the dragon who attempts to destroy her with a flood, but God prepares a place for the woman to escape. The Dragon makes a final attempt to destroy the woman during a period of 1260 days or three and a half years. He sends a flood of people to destroy the woman. But God preserves the woman from the onslaught of the dragon.

Most Bible teachers agree that the child in context is Jesus Christ when he was born as a little child in Bethlehem. Most scholars are in agreement that the Dragon is Satan.

Satan attempted to destroy the child through king Herod.

Jesus offered his life on the cross to save all of mankind from the penalty and the consequences of sin. He rose again on the third day, and is now seated at the right hand of the Father in Heaven.

A lot of discussion and endless speculation has been committed in trying to identify the woman of Revelation 12.

But the two main views are as follows;

IS THE WOMAN THE CHURCH?

The first view is that the woman is the Church.

The view taken is that the Church of Jesus Christ is the persecuted woman.

The dragon is Satan who tries to annihilate the Church.

The problem with this view is quite evident. The woman gives birth to Jesus.

The fact is that the Church did not give birth to Jesus. Jesus brought forth the Church.

Secondly, the Church is a bride who is a virgin. It is a bit odd to present this as a possibility.

IS THE WOMAN ISRAEL?

The second view is that the woman is the "Nation of Israel" who brought forth the Messiah.

When confronted with any scriptures that need more insight, the best possible guidelines we have, are the scriptures itself. We do have a similar incident in the Genesis account of Joseph's dream. In the dream received by Joseph, he dreamt that the sun, moon and eleven stars bowed down to him.

The brothers were indignant and his father Jacob also clearly understood what this meant. He interpreted the sun as himself. The moon as Joseph's mother and the eleven stars are Joseph's brothers.

In the book of Revelation, the woman is clothed with twelve stars which point to the twelve tribes of Israel. The other name given by the Lord to Jacob was Israel. The woman therefore can be identified as the Nation of Israel through whom the Messiah came down to save mankind.

Mary the biological mother of Jesus is an Israelite. The nation of Israel is the woman who was clothed with the sun. She has the moon under her feet and is crowned with twelve stars

THE SECOND SIGN IS THE DRAGON: REVELATION 12:3-4

Then another sign appeared in heaven: and behold, a great red dragon having seven heads and ten horns, and on his heads were seven diadems. And his tail swept away a third of the stars of heaven and threw them to the

earth. And the dragon stood before the woman who was about to give birth, so that when she gave birth, he might devour her child.

We have identified the woman and the child that is born through the woman. The Bible makes it clear that the Dragon is Satan who is also called the Serpent. Satan loses his place in heaven but he has one third of the angels who follow him in his rebellion towards God.

His target is to destroy the woman. Satan has tried through the centuries to destroy Israel.

The Pharaohs of Egypt first tried to destroy the people of Israel. The Assyrians followed and after them, the Babylonians, the Medo-Persians, the Greeks and finally Rome.

Even when they were exiled in other nations, the Jews seemed to invariably find themselves at the receiving end. They were banished from parts of Europe, experienced the Pogroms in Russia and Poland where they had their rights taken away and severely persecuted. The worst horror they faced was when Hitler under demoniac hatred towards them mercilessly massacred over six million Jews.

The Jewish people began to galvanize to get back to the Promised Land under the Zionist movement. The Jewish nation was reborn in 1948. They faced incredible opposition from their Arab neighbors who with a religious zeal continue to challenge their very existence. Although they are relatively secure and a prosperous nation, Satan will instigate a final assault to destroy them in the last days.

The seven heads on the dragon represent the nations which Satan used to destroy Israel.

1. Egypt
2. Assyria
3. Babylon
4. Medo- Persia
5. Greece

6. Rome

7. The Islamic empires which consolidated as the Ottoman Empire.

In the last days, one of these resurrected empires will arise and try and bring about the final destruction of the Jews and the end of Israel as a nation.

The ten horns are the confederacy of ten nations who will join together with the Beast and join him in his plans to destroy the people of God.

REVELATION 12:17

So the dragon was enraged with the woman, and went off to make war with the rest of her children, who keep the commandments of God and hold to the testimony of Jesus.

B. THE BEAST FROM THE SEA

In chapter 13, the book of Revelation introduces us to "The Beast from the Sea."

And the dragon stood on the sand of the seashore.

Then I saw a beast coming up out of the sea, having ten horns and seven heads, and on his horns were ten diadems, and on his heads were blasphemous names. And the beast which I saw was like a leopard, and his feet were like those of a bear, and his mouth like the mouth of a lion. And the dragon gave him his power and his throne and great authority. I saw one of his heads as if it had been slain, and his fatal wound was healed. And the whole earth was amazed and followed after the beast; they worshiped the dragon because he gave his authority to the beast; and they worshiped the beast, saying, "Who is like the beast, and who is able to wage war with him?"

There was given to him a mouth speaking arrogant words and blasphemies, and authority to act for forty-two months was given to him. And he opened his mouth in blasphemies against God, to blaspheme His name and His tabernacle, that is, those who dwell in heaven.

The "Sea" in this context refers to the Mediterranean Sea. It is the only Sea that is connected to Israel. Although the lake of Galilee is mentioned as the "Sea of Galilee", in effect it really is a very large lake.

The Beasts that are mentioned in the book of Daniel and the "Beast from the Sea" mentioned in the book of Revelation are empires that came from this region around the Mediterranean Sea.

What does this mixed animal like creature point towards? The Bible is often laden with typologies in order to bring home the point. To understand these phenomena, we must take the help of Scripture to understand Scripture.

The book of Daniel has world empires represented by animals in Daniel chapter 7.

1. Lion	-	Babylon
2. Bear	-	Medo-Persia
3. Leopard	-	Greece
4. Terrible Beast	-	Rome

Similarly in the book of Revelation, we have not multiple but a single animal shown to us. The difference is that this animal or kingdom is the mixture of all the above. It has the body of a leopard, the mouth of a lion and feet of a bear.

It also has the ten horns that were on the Roman Empire. The Roman Empire had shifted its Capital to Asia Minor in the early 4th Century A.D. Its capital was named Constantinople and was renamed as Istanbul. This was also the capital of the Ottoman Empire which ruled under the banner of the Islamic Caliphate.

The seven heads represent these four kingdoms. It is important to note that the book of Daniel specifies that the Leopard or the Grecian kingdom of Alexander the great had split up into four major parts and came under the rule of his generals after his death at an early age. The book of Daniel describes the Leopard kingdom with four heads. (Daniel 7:6)

That is how we have four kingdoms but seven heads.

The horns on this beast are ten kings that will arise at the end days and align themselves to this "Beast from the Sea."

The kingdom of Babylon had its capital in modern day Iraq but its boundaries extended even till Isarel. The Kingdom of the Medo Persians was predominently Iran but its borders were from parts of India and they also controlled the region of Israel.

The Grecian kingdom extended from Greece going right upto the borders of India. The kingdom of Rome extended through Europe and a large part of the Middle east and northern Africa.

It is important to note that the Roman Empire was split into two parts. The western part of the Empire was overrun by the Barbarian tribes and succumbed to them in the middle of the 5th Century A.D.

The Eastern part of the Empire with its headquarters at Constantinople in morden day Turkey continued on as the Byzantine Empire right upto 1453 A.D.

The eastern part of the empire fell to the onslaught of the Islamic Caliphate.

So this kingdom will be largely in essence, the region that the Leapord kingdom of Greece occupied. The kingdom of Greece extented right from Greece to India. The Lion kingdom is Babylon with its capital in modern day Iraq. The Bear represents the Persian empire with its capital in modern day Iran.

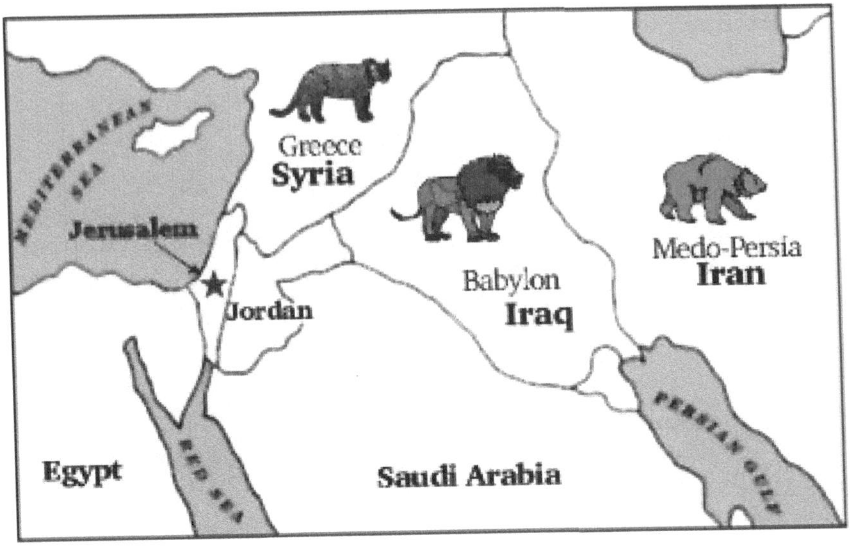

It is extremely crucial to remember that this part of the globe is dominated by one power; Political Islam. Although this region is divided into many nations, the one factor that binds them together is Islam.

The Muslims are awaiting their Messiah who is called the Mahdi whom they claim will one day rule the world under the banner of Islam.

SO WHAT INFORMATION DOES THE WORD OF GOD GIVE US ABOUT THIS KINGDOM?

1. It will be a single kingdom that dominates the earth at the end times.
2. It will comprise of an area predominantly in the Middle East.
3. Satan will give his throne and power to this kingdom.
4. Just as each kingdom was ruled by one supreme authority, so this kingdom will be represented by one king who will do Satan's bidding.
5. This kingdom will be a resurrected kingdom in the sense that it once had power, but lost it. In the last days it will regain power and terrify the people of the Earth.

6. The king of this kingdom will demand the worship of all men of the earth.
7. He will be given authority and rule for a period of forty-two months or three and a half years.
8. He will blaspheme the true God who created the heavens and the earth.
9. He will be given power over the saints and overcome them.
10. He will persecute and seek to destroy the Jewish people as well as those who follow Jesus as the Messiah.
11. The people of the world whose names are not written in the book of life will worship him.

REVELATION 13:7-10

It was also given to him to make war with the saints and to overcome them, and authority over every tribe and people and tongue and nation was given to him. All who dwell on the earth will worship him, everyone whose name has not been written from the foundation of the world in the book of life of the Lamb who has been slain. If anyone has an ear, let him hear. If anyone is destined for captivity, to captivity he goes; if anyone kills with the sword, with the sword he must be killed. Here is the perseverance and the faith of the saints.

THE "LITTLE HORN OF DANIEL CHAPTER 7

The "Little Horn" of Daniel chapter 7 has the same characteristics of "the Beast from the Sea"

1. Both are given authority for a period of three and a half years.
2. Both Blaspheme God.
3. Both demand worship and seek to alter the laws of God.
4. Both are at war with the people of God.

5. Both are in league with ten kings who give their authority to this individual.
6. Both are judged by God and cast into the lake of fire.

It is very clear that they are the same individual.

In the book of Daniel this individual is called the "Little Horn".

In the book of Revelation, he is called "The Beast from the Sea.

C. THE "BEAST FROM THE EARTH"

The Bible also reveals a third character will arise at this point of time. He will be called "The Beast from the Earth.

REVELATION 13:11-17

Then I saw another beast coming up out of the earth; and he had two horns like a lamb and he spoke as a dragon. He exercises all the authority of the first beast in his presence. And he makes the earth and those who dwell in it to worship the first beast, whose fatal wound was healed. He performs great signs, so that he even makes fire come down out of heaven to the earth in the presence of men. And he deceives those who dwell on the earth because of the signs which it was given him to perform in the presence of the beast, telling those who dwell on the earth to make an image to the beast who had the wound of the sword and has come to life.

This individual is also called the "False prophet" in Revelation chapter 19.

He professes to represent Christ but in effect is a spokesman for Satan. He legitimizes the rule of the "Beast" by displaying great signs and wonders in the presence of the people of the earth. He demands that the people of the earth worship the Beast.

Anyone who does not worship the Beast will be dealt with severely. He will control the economy of the earth. Even the purchase of everyday necessities will be allowed only to those who worship and submit to the demand of the beast.

REVELATION 13:15-17

And it was given to him to give breath to the image of the beast, so that the image of the beast would even speak and cause as many as do not worship the image of the beast to be killed. And he causes all, the small and the great, and the rich and the poor, and the freemen and the slaves, to be given a mark on their right hand or on their forehead, and he provides that no one will be able to buy or to sell, except the one who has the mark, either the name of the beast or the number of his name. Here is wisdom. Let him who has understanding calculate the number of the beast, for the number is that of a man; and his number is six hundred and sixty-six.

IDENTIFYING THE BEAST AND HIS NUMBER - 666

The question regarding the meaning of the number 666 or the "number of the Beast" has both fascinated as well as terrified Christians through the centuries.

This number has been attributed to many individuals. Some believe it refers to the Roman Emperor Nero who severely persecuted the Christians in the early church.

Some say it points to the head of the Roman Catholic Church who is the Pope. There is a recorded history of how the Roman Catholic Church has massacred by the millions, the Christians who refused to submit to the authority of the Pope. Some estimates suggest that the number could be between fifty to a hundred million people.

Some say it is Hitler while others say Obama and the list goes on.

THE ORIGIN OF THE NUMBER 666

In order to get a better understanding of the number 666, it is advisable to find out from the past if there is a reference to this number. Since this number is in connection with the act of worship, it is a good starting point.

Only the Living God is worthy of worship. He has created the heavens and the earth along with all life and His power upholds all things. God has also created the Angelic beings.

One among them rebelled against God. The Bible gives him many names. He is Satan.

The Bible also calls him "The Deceiver", The Serpent", The Dragon" etc. He became filled with pride because of the beauty that God had created him with. He desires to be worshipped in the way God is worshipped. From the very beginning he has tried to deceive mankind and sought worship. He has succeeded in blinding the eyes of most of mankind in this regard.

It all started after the flood of Noah. When men began to increase after the flood, they found a leader in a man called Nimrod. The meaning of the word Nimrod means "One who rebels.

He began building cities and the first city he named "Babylon". The meaning of this word means "To confuse or to mix". It was the mixing of the truth with a lie. This was also the first city that was built after the flood during the time of Noah.

It culminated with the building of the tower of Babel. The tower was in the form of an ancient building structure called Ziggurats. The top of these towers was the place where the worship of the starry hosts took place.

It was the starting point of all false religion. This was the worship of created beings and created objects rather than the worship of the Creator. This is where the worship of the sun the moon and the stars began. Any kind of worship that is not presented to the true God, is worship of Satan.

Every false religion has its root and source from Babylon.

In the astrological religion of Babylon, every god had his sacred number or numbers which were often used in place of the god's name. These numbers indicated the god's place and power among the astrological gods...

Because the Babylonians saw their gods as being predominantly evil, they feared that one of them may strike them down sometime.

This is why they made these amulets with a 6 * 6 matrix with the numbers 1 through 36 on them, which are called numeric matrixes magic squares today.

NUMBER OF THE BEAST AMULET.

The design of the amulets was to protect them from a god striking them down using his magic power so the amulets had to be as powerful as possible.

In order to increase its power, they arranged these numbers in such a way that the sum of any given row, column or diagonal was 111, and therefore the sum of all six rows or all six columns was 666.

6	32	3	34	35	1
7	11	27	28	8	30
19	14	16	15	23	24
18	20	22	21	17	13
25	29	10	9	26	12
36	5	33	4	2	31

THE BABYLONIAN RELIGIOUS SYSTEM

In this system of worship, they had 36 supreme gods, which included the sun god, which they believed to be the father of all the other gods and so was supreme over all.

The Babylonians believed that numbers had power over their gods they worshiped so they assigned numbers to their gods so that they could have power over them.

They did this by counting their gods and assigning a consecutive number to each of the 36 lesser supreme gods, and then added up these numbers (from 1 to 36) and assigned the sum to the sun god.

The sun god was assigned number 1 as it was the father of all gods and thus was also the male deity. The moon god was assigned number 2 and of course was the female deity. The gods numbered from 3 through 36 were considered the children of the sun and the moon god.

THE "MARK" ON THE HAND OR FOREHEAD

How is the mark of the beast placed on someone's right hand or forehead? (Revelation 13:16)

Regarding his commands to the nation of Israel regarding his Word, God said: "Bind them as a reminder on your hand, and they should be like a headband on your forehead." (Deuteronomy 11:18)

This meant that the Israelites were not to literally mark their hands and foreheads, but that God's words would guide all their actions and thoughts.

Likewise, rather than being something literal such as a 666 tattoo, the mark of the beast symbolically identifies those who let the political and religious system rule their lives.

Those with the mark of the beast place themselves in opposition to God. (Revelation 14:9, 10; 19:19-21.

SO WHAT CLUES DO WE HAVE

1. The "Beast" is a person whose kingdom is predominantly in the region of the Middle East.
2. It is not only a political power but also a religious power.
3. The system of worship is of Babylonian origin.

4. The symbol of the Babylonian form of worship was the Sun and the Moon.
5. There is a power in this region which ticks all the boxes. This power already rules in this region. It is political Islam.
6. Wherever Islam is the majority even today, it totally dominates the lives of the people. Islam demands complete submission and freedom of religion is negligible.
7. The symbol of Islam is the Sun and the half Moon which is the Babylonian system of worship.

Do we have any more information on this topic? Can we consider extra biblical sources for more insight? These are important questions.

There is interesting information we get about the topic of the number 666. Just like the study on the "End Times" is part of our endeavor to understand the future, the Muslims also are keenly awaiting their own Messiah called the Mahdi. It is intriguing as to how the hero of the Bible is the villain in the Quran. And the villain of the Bible is the hero in Islam.

The following information is derived from Islamic sources.

There are **three Signs** for Muslims of the end of History - each is a Man.

1. THE MAHDI – ISLAMIC MESSIAH

After reviewing the various Islamic traditions and opinions of the Muslim scholars, let's now review and walk through a list of what we have learned about the person and the mission of the Mahdi as he exists in the minds of many of the 1.8 billion Muslims worldwide.

The Mahdi is Islam's primary messiah figure. He will be a descendant of Muhammad and will bear Muhammad's name (Muhammad bin Abdullah). He will be the Caliph and Imam (vice-regent and leader) of Muslims worldwide. He will appear riding a white horse (possibly symbolic). He will have supernatural power from Allah over the wind and the rain and crops.

The Mahdi will be an unparalleled spiritual, political and military world leader who will emerge after a period of great turmoil and suffering upon the earth. He will establish justice and righteousness throughout the world and eradicate tyranny and oppression. He will possess and distribute enormous amounts of wealth and will be loved by all the people of the earth. He will lead a world revolution and establish a new world order. The Mahdi will lead military action against all those who oppose him and will invade many countries.

He will cause Islam to be the only religion practiced on the earth. He will establish the new Islamic world headquarters from Jerusalem. According to Islamic sources he will rule for seven years (possibly as much as eight or nine).

He will make a seven-year peace treaty with a Jew of priestly lineage. He will obtain some previously undiscovered biblical manuscripts with which he will use to argue with the Jews and cause some Jews to convert to Islam. He will also re-discover the Ark of the Covenant from the Sea of Galilee, which he will bring to Jerusalem.

He will conquer Israel for Islam and lead the "faithful Muslims" in a final slaughter/battle against the Jews.

2. THE ISLAMIC "JESUS"

Muslims revere Jesus (whom they call Isa) as the Masih or Messiah. In Islamic eschatology, the Mahdi will arrive at the same time that Isa returns. He is a prophet.

Isa will descend to earth in Syria, east of Damascus, dressed in yellow robes, and will assist the Mahdi, who will rule over the world for seven years (or, in some Islamic traditions, nine or 19 years). He will come back on the wing of two angels who flew him down to meet the gathering of the army of the Mahdi.

He will pray to the Mahdi- call him "Lord."

He will make a pilgrimage to Mecca and will establish world- wide Sharia law.

He will be the greatest Muslim Evangelist. He will reveal to the Christians that they were deceived.

That he never really died for their sins. He will shatter crosses, and abolish the tax on "non-Muslims" because there won't be any people who practice any other faith.

At the end of the Mahdi's rule, there will be a day of Judgment for the entire human race.

He will kill the "Islamic Anti-Christ."

The parallels between the biblical Antichrist and the Mahdi of Islam are chilling. Both are associated with the End Times and the Judgment. Both are said to possess political, military and religious power, and head up a one-world religion. The Mahdi will force all non-Muslim people to convert to Islam. Like the Antichrist, the Mahdi will establish Jerusalem as his capital, from which he will rule the Earth.

3. THE ISLAMIC "ANTI-CHRIST"

He is called "DAJAL"- the great deceiver. He comes on a mule to earth and is blind in one eye. He is an Infidel but who also does miracles.

He claims to be Jesus- "The son of God" and will attempt to stop the Mahdi and the "true Jesus". But the "Islamic Jesus" will kill him.

Although some of the above points do not concur with the Biblical description of Jesus, some key elements regarding the persona of Jesus are included here.

WHAT CAN WE LEARN FROM THIS?

1. The Biblical Jesus is the Islamic "Anti-Christ"

2. The Biblical Anti-Christ is the Islamic "Redeemer"

3. The Biblical "False Prophet" is the Islamic Jesus.

This does fit the Biblical narrative too, but in reverse. Is this all-mere coincidence?

There will be great battle. But the Jesus of the bible will rule forever.

It is important to remember that the Muslims are sincere and most of them are like people of other religions. But we would be naïve if we do not know the reality of the reason why so many hold on to the ideology of militant Islam. Islam is not just a religion but also a political religion. There is no division between the state and religion.

The Bible is the only source where we can be 100% sure about any subject. It is our guiding light. Only in the light of God's word can we find truth. If any other source is in agreement and does not violate any commands of God or His teaching, then it is can be referred to. However, the greatest care must be taken to see that we weigh everything in life from the context of the word of God rather than extraneous sources.

THE "MAN OF SIN"

The Bible warns us that the return of Jesus will not take place until the "Man of Sin" or the Anti-Christ reveals himself. He will rule from the Temple (or in the area where the Temple existed) and demand the worship of all mankind. He will not only have military strength but display great signs and wonders.

2 THESSALONIANS 2:1-4

Now we request you, brethren, with regard to the coming of our Lord Jesus Christ and our gathering together to Him, that you not be quickly shaken from your composure or be disturbed either by a spirit or a message or a letter as if from us, to the effect that the day of the Lord has come. Let no one in any way deceive you, for it will not come unless the apostasy comes first, and the man of lawlessness is revealed, the son of destruction, who opposes and exalts himself above every so-called god or object of worship, so that he takes his seat in the temple of God, displaying himself as being God.

1 THESSALONIANS 2:6-11

And you know what restrains him now, so that in his time he will be revealed. For the mystery of lawlessness is already at work; only he who now restrains will do so until he is taken out of the way. Then that lawless one will be revealed whom the Lord will stay with the breath of His mouth and bring to an end by the appearance of His coming; that is, the one who's coming is in accord with the activity of Satan, with all power and signs and false wonders, and with all the deception of wickedness for those who perish, because they did not receive the love of the truth so as to be saved. For this reason, God will send upon them a deluding influence so that they will believe what is false, in order that they all may be judged who did not believe the truth, but took pleasure in wickedness.

THE ALLIANCE THAT PERSECUTES THE PEOPLE OF GOD

We are now in a position to summarize this alliance.

Satan is the Dragon who opposes the people of God and his agenda is to destroy them. At a certain point in time, when he is cast out of heaven, he will try and destroy the people of God with a vengeance.

He will unleash the "Beast from the Sea" to whom he will give his throne and authority. He will also demand the worship of the people of the earth through his puppet "The False prophet. They will blaspheme God and oppress the people of God.

We find that in the book of Revelation in Chapter 19, the beast and his armies are gathered together to destroy God's people and to fight against Jesus.

Jesus however will defeat them and cast the Beast and the False Prophet into the lake of fire.

Satan will be bound and cast into the Abyss where he will remain a thousand years.

CHAPTER 7

IDENTIFYING THE "ANTI-CHRIST"

The Antichrist is the opposite of Christ. Just as Christ came to earth to do God's will; the Antichrist will come to do the will of Satan. He will be Satan manifest in the form of man.

The Greek word used here for "Antichrist" can have two meanings. First, it can mean "against Christ," in the sense of someone or some power who opposes Christ and His work.

Second, the word can mean "instead of Christ," signifying a person or power who takes the place of Christ—a counterfeit Christ.

Satan's whole ambition is to be like God in power and glory, and he works for this with all of his might, night and day. His intention is to replace God, and he will send the Antichrist as a means to do so. The Antichrist will proclaim himself as God, and assert himself as ruler of this world.

But what kind of a world would be willing to accept the emissary of Satan as Lord? Is it possible that this world we live in now has come to such a state?

THE SPIRIT OF ANTICHRIST

The prevailing spirit in the world is the spirit of Antichrist, which has been working since the earliest days of the Church. The spirit of Antichrist can be summed up as every spirit that does not confess that Jesus Christ has come in the flesh.

1 JOHN 4:1-3

Beloved, do not believe every spirit, but test the spirits to see whether they are from God, because many false prophets have gone out into the world. By this you know the Spirit of God: every spirit that confesses that Jesus Christ has come in the flesh is from God; and every spirit that does not confess Jesus is not from God; this is the spirit of the antichrist, of which you have heard that it is coming, and now it is already in the world.

2 JOHN 1:7

"For many deceivers have gone out into the world who do not confess Jesus Christ as coming in the flesh. This is a deceiver and an antichrist"

According to God's Word, these antichrists in the early church were counterfeit Christians who had split away from the body of true believers. They were deceivers who had not really experienced a genuine gospel conversion. They were liars who denied that Jesus was the promised Messiah.

1 JOHN 2:22

"Who is a liar but he who denies that Jesus is the Christ? He is antichrist who denies the Father and the Son."

The spirit of Antichrist denies the relationship between the Father and His son Jesus. It attacks the reality of the death and resurrection of Jesus. The Bible declares that Jesus is the "Son of God" who came to earth as the "Son of Man" – fully God and fully human. He was born in human likeness and paid the price for the sins of all mankind. Now he is seated at the right hand of the Father and is worshipped by the hosts of heaven.

So which religion stands directly in conflict with the most fundamental truth of the Bible?

It is the religion of Islam.

Islam accepts the virgin birth of Jesus and He is held in high regard by the Muslims. He is acknowledged as a prophet and a wise teacher. It records that Jesus was a miracle worker and that He ascended to heaven.

But the most fundamental truth that Jesus declared about himself is what Islam rejects. The fact that Jesus is the "Son of God. It also denies that Jesus died on the cross or rose again from the dead. The Jesus of the Quran is very different to the Jesus of the Bible

Let's review what information we have regarding the Spirit of the Antichrist

1. It denies that Jesus is the Messiah

2. It denies that Jesus is the "Son of God"

WAS THE EARLY CHURCH EXPECTING THE ANTI-CHRIST?

1 JOHN 2:18

"Dear children, this is the last hour; and as you have heard that the antichrist is coming, even now many antichrists have come. This is how we know it is the last hour."

In this verse, God is speaking to the early Christian church. Obviously, the word hour is used in a figurative sense. The same Greek word is often translated as "time;" in fact, that is how the King James Version of the Bible translates it in this same verse. God is stating that humanity is living in the last time, the last era, and the last period of earth's history.

God is reminding the early church believers of a prophecy they had already heard—namely, that the antichrist was going to come.

God also says that in addition to the coming of "the" antichrist—a special antichrist—will arise in the last days.

The spirit of Antichrist was already at work from the beginning of church history and many individuals rose up against Christ as antichrists. The Bible warns us that in the last days, one individual who will personify everything that is against Christ will rise up to persecute the people of God.

MAN OF LAWLESSNESS

2 THESSALONIANS 2:1-2

Now we request you, brethren, with regard to the coming of our Lord Jesus Christ and our gathering together to Him, that you not be quickly shaken from your composure or be disturbed either by a spirit or a message or a letter as if from us, to the effect that the day of the Lord has come.

There was much scope for speculations and false teaching of the return of the Lord as the Church grew exponentially in the early days. One such teaching that had begun to be propagated was, that the day of the Lord had already come. Paul wrote to the Thessalonians church that prior to the coming of the Lord they would see certain situations developing.

The first sign given to the church was that they there would be a great falling away from the faith because of deception. It would come through a person the Bible calls – the man of lawlessness. This man is also doomed to destruction. He will exalt himself over every God or object of worship. He will demand that the world worships him.

2 THESSALONIANS 2:3-6

Let no one in any way deceive you, for it will not come unless the apostasy comes first, and the man of lawlessness is revealed, the son of destruction, who opposes and exalts himself above every so-called god or object of worship, so that he takes his seat in the temple of God, displaying himself as being God. Do you not remember that while I was still with you, I was telling you these things?

And you know what restrains him now, so that in his time he will be revealed. For the mystery of lawlessness is already at work; only he who now restrains will do so until he is taken out of the way.

In this profound prophecy of last-day events, the Bible says that there is going to be a rebellion, an apostasy, a great falling away from the faith. In conjunction with this apostasy, the "man of lawlessness"—also known as "the antichrist" and the "man of sin"—will be revealed. This Antichrist will set himself up in God's temple and counterfeit the ministry of Jesus.

He will rule from the area in Jerusalem where the Temple of God existed declaring himself as God. He will come in the power of Satan with a great display of signs and false wonders. He will be hugely successful in deceiving with great depths of wickedness, men who choose to reject the truth. Those who hate the truth will gladly accept the lies of this evil despot.

2 THESSALONIANS 2:9-10

.... the one whose coming is in accord with the activity of Satan, with all power and signs and false wonders, 10 and with all the deception of wickedness for those who perish, because they did not receive the love of the truth so as to be saved.

2 THESSALONIANS 2:11-12

For this reason, God will send upon them a deluding influence so that they will believe what is false, in order that they all may be judged who did not believe the truth, but took pleasure in wickedness.

God desires that all men would come to Him for salvation as he loves each person whom He has created. He has reached out to rebellious man through His Son Jesus to bring us back to Him. But consistent rejection of His love can harden the heart of men. When God gives up on any man it is tragic. Here we see that since men would not accept the truth, they were allowed to be deceived.

THE DESTRUCTION OF THE ANTICHRIST

2 THESSALONIANS 2:8

Then that lawless one will be revealed whom the Lord will slay with the breath of His mouth and bring to an end by the appearance of His coming;

The man of sin will be destroyed when the Lord Jesus arrives. The Antichrist is only powerful in as much as the lord allows him to be. When Jesus arrives, he will put an end to this evil person. Darkness can never overcome light.

JESUS HAS WARNED THE CHURCH IN ADVANCE

MATTHEW 24:4, 5, 23-26

"Watch out that no one deceives you. For many will come in my name, claiming, 'I am the Christ,' and will deceive many. . .. At that time if anyone says to you, 'Look, here is the Christ!' or, 'There he is!' do not believe it. For false Christs and false prophets will appear and perform great signs and miracles to deceive even the elect—if that were possible.

Interestingly Jesus points to the above situation that will occur at the time of the great tribulation that will come upon the nation of Israel as well as the whole earth.

The Abomination that causes desolation is the sign that the last days will have begun. (Matthew 24:15) The Abomination is the blasphemous event that will take place on the area of the Temple which is the Holy place. It is at the time when the Antichrist begins his rule from Jerusalem at the Temple mount proclaiming himself as God and demanding worship.

CAN WE IDENTIFY THE ANTICHRIST?

The Bible gives us clear information to help us identify the Antichrist. The first real confrontation with this entity is in the book of Daniel (Chapter 7).

The prophet Daniel was shown dreams and visions of four beasts that arose from the Sea. The four beasts are four kingdoms that would arise that would rule over the nation of Israel. We have earlier already identified these four kingdoms.

The visions further reveal to Daniel that just before the return of Jesus, ten kings would arise and after them another king would arise.

The Bible calls this king – "The Little Horn"

This king will speak against God and persecute the saints of God. He will denounce the commands of God and rule for a period of three and a half years.

This demoniac ruler will be judged by God and his dominion will be taken away, annihilated and destroyed forever.

Then the sovereignty, the dominion and the greatness of all the kingdoms under the whole heaven will be given to the people of the saints of God. The kingdom of Jesus will be an everlasting kingdom and all the dominions will serve and obey Him. (Daniel 7:24-27)

LET'S TAKE A CLOSER LOOK AT THE "LITTLE HORN"

- The "Little horn" will arise just prior to the return of the Lord Jesus.
- He will speak blasphemy against God.
- He will persecute the saints of God.
- He will denounce the commands of God.
- He will rule for a period of "time, times and a half time" (3.5 years)
- He will be slain and cast into the fire.

THE GEOGRAPHICAL AREA FROM WHERE THE ANTICHRIST WILL ARISE

In the book of Revelation, we come face to face with this same entity but this time he has a new name. In Revelation 13, he is called - "The Beast from the Sea."

We will trace the geographical area from where this beast will arise.

We must follow the Biblical trend of identifying the beast. In Daniel Chapter 7, beasts are kingdoms. But each kingdom has a ruler. For example, the Beast kingdom of Babylon was represented by the lion but the ruler was king Nebuchadnezzar.

The "Beast from the Sea" looks like a Leopard but has the mouth of a lion and the feet of a bear.

The Leopard kingdom was Greece which stretched from Greece to India including all of the Middle East and North Africa.

The Lion represented the kingdom of Babylon with its capital in modern Iraq and the bear represented Persia with its capital in modern day Iran. It also had ten horns which represented the kingdom of Rome.

But we must remember that Rome was divided into two parts. It had the western part in Europe and the eastern part with its capital in modern day Turkey. The eastern part of the empire lasted almost 1000 years after the western part of the empire had collapsed.

Keeping in line with the area that we need to focus on, it is clear that this beast is from the Middle East region.
What dominates this area? – Political Islam.

LET'S TAKE A CLOSE LOOK AT THE "BEAST FROM THE SEA"

- This beast has seven heads, ten horns with seven crowns.
- The heads had blasphemous names.
- Looks like a Leopard with feet of a bear and mouth of a lion.

- The dragon gave him his power, throne and great authority.
- One of its head had a fatal wound which was healed.
- The whole earth was amazed and followed the beast.
- The people of the earth worshipped the beast and were afraid of it.
- The beast spoke arrogant words and blasphemed God.
- The beast was given authority to rule for forty-two months (3.5 years)
- He will wage war with the saints of God and overcome them during this period.
- Everyone whose name is not written in the book of life will worship him.

FROM WHERE WILL THIS BEAST GET HIS AUTHORITY?

The dragon whom the Bible calls Satan will give the beast his throne and authority. Interestingly when John wrote a letter to the church at Pergamum, it is revealed that Satan's throne was in Pergamum (Revelation chapter 2). Pergamum is in modern day Turkey. Whether we can use this as a clue is subject to discussion. At least during the 1st century, Satan had made this area his residence.

THE FALSE PROPHET WHO ASSISTS THE ANTICHRIST REVELATION 13:11-18

The Antichrist will not be alone in this endeavor to deceive mankind. He will receive assistance from another individual whom the Bible calls "The beast from the earth. "This beast has two horns like a lamb but he speaks the language of the Dragon. He will pretend to represent Jesus but will in-fact follow the agenda of Satan.

- He exercises all the authority of the Antichrist
- He makes the earth and those who dwell in it worship the Antichrist.

- He performs great signs, even makes fire come down from heaven to the earth.
- He deceives those who dwell on earth and causes them to make an image of the beast.
- He gives breath to the image of the beast.
- Those who refuse to bow down to this image will be killed.
- He forces men to be given a mark of the beast on their right hand or forehead.
- He enforces the rule that no one will be able to buy or sell without the mark.

IS THE ANTICHRIST A NORMAL HUMAN BEING?

Satan has used ordinary human beings throughout history to do his bidding. He has endowed them with his power and authority. At the beginning of His ministry on earth, Jesus was tempted by Satan. His offer was that Jesus would be given the kingdoms of the earth and their glory if Jesus bowed down to him. He claimed that it was his to give as it was handed over to him. (Luke 4:5-8)

Although Jesus refused Satan's offer, he did not dismiss Satan's claim of having domain over the kingdoms of the earth. This domain was given by God to Adam and Eve. When Adam sinned against God, they lost authority and Satan gained dominion. For now, Satan continues to use human rulers as puppets to rule over the earth. This will continue until Jesus returns and the kingdoms of the earth become the kingdom of our God.

For Satan's final stand against the kingdom of God, he will use the Antichrist who is different from the kings whom Satan has used earlier.

As we continue to study the book of Revelation, we find that in Chapter nine, the fifth trumpet is blown by an angel.

John saw that a star from heaven had fallen to the earth. (This refers to a fallen angel).

A key to the bottomless pit was given to this angel. The angel opened the bottomless pit and smoke like one from a great furnace went up from the pit. Out of the smoke came locusts upon the earth.

The description is that of a huge demoniac invasion upon the earth. They are led by a king who is the angel of the abyss. His name in Hebrew is Abaddon which means "The angel of death".

In the Greek he has a name – Apollyon which means "The Destroyer"

THE BEAST FROM THE ABYSS KILLS THE TWO WITNESSES

During the time of the great tribulation when the Antichrist rules from Jerusalem, God will raise up two witnesses who will testify to the world and prophecy to the world. They will have power to shut up the sky so that no rain falls during the days that of their prophetic ministry. They have the authority to display God's power and witness about the true God. They will prophecy for a period of 1260 days (3.5 years).

After they have finished their testimony, the beast that comes out of the Abyss will make war with them and kill them.

Is the Antichrist also the beast from the Abyss? We will need to get more details.

THE SCARLET BEAST AND "MYSTERY BABYLON."

In Revelation chapter 17, we are introduced to two new characters.

- The women called "Mystery Babylon"
- The Scarlet beast

REVELATION 17:1-3

Then one of the seven angels who had the seven bowls came and spoke with me, saying, "Come here, I will show you the judgment of the great harlot who sits on many waters, with whom the kings of the earth committed acts of immorality, and those who dwell on the earth were made drunk with the wine of her immorality."

And he carried me away in the Spirit into a wilderness; and I saw a woman sitting on a scarlet beast, full of blasphemous names, having seven heads and ten horns.

MYSTERY BABYLON

- She was seated on the scarlet beast - Verse 3
- The woman was clothed in great riches - Verse 4
- She had a cup full of immorality and abominations - Verse 5
- Her description - "Babylon the great, - Verse 5
  - The mother of harlots
  - And of the abominations of the earth.
- She was drunk with the blood of God's people - Verse 6
- The woman is the great city which rules over the kings of the earth - Verse 18

The woman represents false religion that is a direct rebellion against the Creator. Men began to worship creation rather than the Creator. The religion of Babylon was the worship of the sun, moon and the stars. Idolatry and the occult followed.

The symbol of Babylon is the sun and the half moon.

THE SCARLET BEAST

- "The beast that you saw was, - Verse 8

  - And is not,

  - And is about to come up out

- The beast is about to come from the Abyss - Verse 8
- The Beast will be destroyed -Verse 8
- Those whose names are not written in the book of life - Verse 8

  - Will be amazed at the beast
- The seven heads are seven mountains - Verse 9
- The woman has been sitting on these mountains. - Verse 9
- They are also seven kings or kingdoms. - Verse 10
- Five have fallen - (Egypt, Assyria, Babylon, Persia, Greece) - Verse 10

  One is – (Rome)

  One is to come – The Islamic Ottoman Empire
- The beast which was and is not, is the eighth kingdom - Verse 11

  This eighth kingdom is from among the first seven.
- The ten horns are ten kings that have not received a kingdom- Verse 12

  They will receive authority for a short very short of time.

  Their purpose is to give their power and authority to the beast.
- The beast hates the woman and will destroy her. - Verse 16
- The Beast will wage war against Jesus who will defeat them - Verse 14

As the book of Revelation unfolds, it becomes evidently clear that the "Beast from the sea" of Revelation 13, is the same entity as the "Little Horn" of Daniel 7.

What also becomes evident is that the "Scarlet beast" and the "beast from the sea" are the same kingdom, led by the same person.

The "Scarlet beast" comes out from the Abyss. (Revelation 17:8)

Putting these facts together we can summarize what we have learned so far.

We are very close to the return of Jesus. But before He returns, the earth will go through major turmoil. Satan knows his time is near and so he will up the ante. He will bring forth the Antichrist who will oppose the true God. He will be allowed dominion for three and a half years. He will deceive the world along with the false prophet. The people of Israel will be severely tested and all of God's people will have to take a stand for Jesus.

Those who do not receive the true light will be deceived and join the darkness.

With eternity at stake, it is time to wake up!!

REVELATION 19:19

And I saw the beast and the kings of the earth and their armies assembled to make war against Him who sat on the horse and against His arm.Doom of the Beast and False Prophet

DOOM OF THE BEAST AND FALSE PROPHET

REVELATION 19:20-21

And the beast was seized, and with him the false prophet who performed the signs in his presence, by which he deceived those who had received the mark of the beast and those who worshiped his image; these two were thrown alive into the lake of fire which burns with brimstone. And the rest were killed with the sword which came from the mouth of Him who sat on the horse, and all the birds were filled with their flesh

The summary of these world kingdoms.

Daniel 2 (Statue Dream)	Daniel 7 (Daniel's Beasts)	Revelation 17 (Seven Headed Beast
		Egypt 2100-1400BC
		Assyria 1100-605BC
Gold	Lion	Babylon 605 - 538BC

Silver	Bear	Medo-Persia 538-333BC
Brass	Leopard	Greece 333-146BC
Iron	Terrifying Beast	Rome 27BC-1453AD
Iron & Clay feet	Trampled Daniel's people until 1948	Yet to come (Ottoman 1299-1923)
Iron & Clay toes	10 horns & Little horn	10 king coalition led by the eighth from among the seven
God will set up an eternal kingdom	Everlasting dominion of the One like a son of man	God & the Lamb shall reign for ever and ever (Rev 22)

CHAPTER 8

THE CITY OF BABYLON AND THE SCARLET BEAST

In the book of Revelation, we have two cities that represent two different powers.

Both cities are represented by women who are radically different.

THE TWO WOMEN OF REVELATION

1. The pure bride- New Jerusalem
2. The filthy prostitute –Mystery Babylon

THESE ARE THE TWO CITIES.

One represents a rebellious city.

The other is the "city of God"

In the Bible, cities are not very good places. It is first mentioned that Lamech built cities and then he forged weapons of destruction. Cities came through Lamech who is a descendant of Cain and so came from a wicked family line.

THE TOWER OF BABEL.

The city that challenged God was the city of Babylon or Babel built on the banks of the Euphrates River. It was built by a man named Nimrod who was a mighty hunter. He wanted to build the tallest building in the world. He wanted to build a building that reached up- to the heavens, but had been built by human hands.

Nimrod gathered the people of the Earth to build a tower.

Since he was building in Mesopotamia and no stone was available, he built it out of bricks (made out of clay). They built a stepped tower, a man-made mountain.

God dealt with this rebellion by confusing their language.

People spoke in different languages and could not understand each other and sounded like they were babbling. That's where the word Babel came from.

In the Chinese alphabet you find the entire book of genesis 1-11 right up to the tower of Babel.

Chinese is a pictorial language. Interestingly the Chinese letter for the word boat is a boat with eight people. The Chinese word for temptation is a garden with two trees. This is a real indication that as the Lord confused the language of the people at the Tower of Babel, they scattered to all the parts of the earth. But they carried with them the knowledge of the creation, the fall of Man as well as the great flood of Noah.

Cities have to be built near river bodies for easy transportation. Babylon became a mighty city and a great empire and Nebuchadnezzar at one time ruled over it. He became a believer in God. But Babylon became an enemy of Jerusalem. The city of Jerusalem and the first Jewish temple were both destroyed by Babylon.

The Babylon of the book of Revelation is not the same city. It represents the same spiritual climate that was present at the real city of Babylon.

The Babylon of Revelation is a coastal city with ships passing by. The book of Revelation warns people to flee from Babylon as its destruction is near.

MYSTERY BABYLON OF REVELATION: REVELATION 17:1-6

Then one of the seven angels who had the seven bowls came and spoke with me, saying, "Come here, I will show you the judgment of the great harlot who sits on many waters, with whom the kings of the earth committed acts of immorality, and those who dwell on the earth were made drunk with the wine of her immorality.

" And he carried me away in the Spirit into a wilderness; and I saw a woman sitting on a scarlet beast, full of blasphemous names, having seven heads and ten horns. The woman was clothed in purple and scarlet, and adorned with gold and precious stones and pearls, having in her hand a gold cup full of abominations and of the unclean things of her immorality,

and on her forehead a name was written, a mystery,

"BABYLON THE GREAT, THE MOTHER OF HARLOTS AND OF THE ABOMINATIONS OF THE EARTH. "And I saw the woman drunk with the blood of the saints, and with the blood of the witnesses of Jesus. When I saw her, I wondered greatly. 7

There have been many Babylon's. But the Babylon of Revelation is the city which now rules over the kings of the earth. Babylon is a prostitute. She has sold a lie to the nations and has profited by her trade. She is drunk on the blood of the saints. It is a city of pleasure and money.

DESCRIPTION OF BABYLON:

- She is a prostitute.
- She is seated on many waters.
- The kings of the earth have committed sexual immorality with her.
- Woman arrayed in purple and scarlet.
- Adorned with gold jewels and pearls.
- Holds a golden cup – full of abomination and then implodes in her sexual immorality.
- Drunk with the blood of saints.

WHICH CITY COULD REPRESENT THE BABYLON OF REVELATION?

The identity of this city has been a difficult task.

Suggestions regarding its identity range from Rome, to Washington D.C to Mecca as well as other cities.

Some believe it is modern Germany. Germany is making an effort to become the financial capital of Europe at Frankfurt. They have built a vast new stock exchange. Outside the exchange is a huge golden calf. In the bank headquarters a massive painting around the wall is the picture of hell. Every known sin is portrayed in this painting which is full of demons gloating over their victims.

There are bronze figures standing near the cash counters all totally naked in and in objectionable poses. Businesses control the nation.

IS IT ROME?

The Catholic Church has the blood of millions of Bibles believing disciples of Jesus on its hands. It is a historical reality that during the dark ages, it actively sought to keep the Bible from the hands of ordinary people. Entire groups of people were massacred under the guidance of the Popes if they did not submit to the dictates of the Catholic Church.

Historical data point to the number of people killed during the inquisitions from fifty to a hundred million Christians.

It is a godless city. Rome is the first city which Peter calls Babylon.

"The church that is in Babylon sends greeting." (1 Peter 5:13)

COULD BABYLON BE IN THE MIDDLE EAST?

The Middle East is responsible for the martyrdom of many Christians.

The city of Mecca is the head - quarters of the Islamic world.

There are some interesting facts about Mecca.

- Mecca means "Mother" (Babylon is called "Mother of harlots")
- Mecca is the center for radical Muslims who regularly slaughter Christian populations.
- The key figures of the Babylonian system of worship are the sun, moon and stars.
- The Islamic flag is the half - crescent moon and the sun.
- The believers were beheaded for the Testimony of Jesus Beheading is still followed in Saudi.

WHO IS THE BEAST THAT THE HARLOT IS SITTING ON?
REVELATION 17:7-8

And the angel said to me, "Why do you wonder? I will tell you the mystery of the woman and of the beast that carries her, which has the seven heads and the ten horns.

"The beast that you saw was, and is not, and is about to come up out of the abyss and go to destruction. And those who dwell on the earth, whose name has not been written in the book of life from the foundation of the world, will wonder when they see the beast, that he was and is not and will come.

The Scarlet Beast has seven heads and ten horns. It is interesting to note that the "Beast from the Sea" also has seven heads and ten horns. The other common trait is that they were both in power once but have lost their power. They will now arise from the ashes.

They are one and the same power. The "Beast from the Sea" shows us the location or the extent of the rule of this power.

The Scarlet Beast reveals that this power is not only a political power but also a religious power.

Another interesting fact is that the ruler of this kingdom comes out of the Abyss. It is not just a human being but a supernatural being that is evil. When we read through the description of the kingdoms from the book of Daniel Chapter 2, we find that the latter end of the kings is represented by the ten toes and the feet. The ten toes and feet are made of a mixture of iron and clay. And then the Bible points out to something different about this coalition.

DANIEL 2:43

And in that you saw the iron mixed with common clay, they will combine with one another in the seed of men; but they will not adhere to one another, even as iron does not combine with pottery.

What is this mixture and why does the Bible talk about mixing with the seed of men?

Who or what mixes with the seed of men?

There is one period of time recorded in the bible in the 6th chapter of Genesis, that we come across a similar situation. In this passage the Bible records a period of time when the fallen angels began to have sexual relationships with human beings. This brought about children who were a hybrid of semi human beings. Immorality and evil sky rocketed and God had to send the great flood during the time of Noah because mankind had become completely wicked.

(REVELATION 17:9-13)

Here is the mind which has wisdom. The seven heads are seven mountains on which the woman sits, and they are seven kings; five have fallen, one is, the other has not yet come; and when he comes, he must remain a little while. The beast which was and is not, is himself also an eighth and is one of the seven, and he goes to destruction. The ten horns which you saw are ten kings who have not yet received a kingdom, but they receive authority as kings with the beast for one hour. These have one purpose, and they give their power and authority to the beast.

The beast is seated on seven mountains which are seven kingdoms. Five have fallen, one is and the other has not yet come. The seventh kingdom would come after the sixth. All these kingdoms have ruled over the territory or the people of Israel at some time in history.

John the apostle was writing the book of Revelation in the latter part of the 1st Century A.D. He was also writing at the time that the Romans ruled over that part of the world. So, which were the five kingdoms before the Romans?

These five have fallen - Egypt, Assyria, Babylon, Medo-Persia, Greece.

One is - Rome

The other has not yet come - Ottoman Empire whose capital was in modern Turkey.

All these kingdoms had one thing in common.

All were under the influence of the woman "Mystery Babylon. All these kingdoms followed and propagated the Babylonian religion of Satan. These kingdoms have at some point in history attempted to destroy the people of God.

The Bible considers the people of God as both the believers of Jesus Christ as well the Jewish people. The Jewish people lost their land as they rejected the Messiah.

But God has not finished with them yet. The book of Romans makes this point very clear.

The Jewish people were not living in the Promised Land during the Ottoman Empire, and were therefore not in much danger from this empire. But it is interesting to note that the Ottoman Empire was on the side of Nazi Germany even as Hitler attempted to annihilate the Jews.

The entire area where the Ottoman Empire expanded under the banner of Islam was predominately Christian. The Christians were subjugated through terror and economic hardships by the Islamic rulers. In just a little over hundred years Islam spread through the power of the sword all the way from Spain in Europe, to India and even parts of the former Soviet Union.

The eighth Kingdom will be a future kingdom that rules once again.

It will arise from among the seven earlier kingdoms.

We can say with a certain amount of predictability at this current point in world history that this empire will be an Islamic Caliphate that arises once again.

THE BEAST DESTROYS BABYLON- REVELATION 17:15-18

And he said to me, "The waters which you saw where the harlot sits, are peoples and multitudes and nations and tongues. And the ten horns which you saw, and the beast, these will hate the harlot and will make her desolate and naked, and will eat her flesh and will burn her up with fire.

For God has put it in their hearts to execute His purpose by having a common purpose, and by giving their kingdom to the beast, until the words of God will be fulfilled.

The woman whom you saw is the great city, which reigns over the kings of the earth."

The ten kings will give their authority to the Beast. This alliance will then attempt to make war with the Lamb of God who is Jesus. But will utterly fail against Jesus who is the King of Kings.

But before this they will destroy the city of Babylon.

She is also called the Harlot. So now we need to identify this city who the Bible calls "mystery Babylon. We get to know more about this city in Chapter 18

REVELATION 18: 9-13

"And the kings of the earth, who committed acts of immorality and lived sensuously with her, will weep and lament over her when they see the smoke of her burning, 10 standing at a distance because of the fear of her torment, saying, 'Woe, woe, the great city, Babylon, the strong city! For in one hour your judgment has come.'

11 "And the merchants of the earth weep and mourn over her, because no one buys their cargoes any more— cargoes of gold and silver and precious stones and pearls and fine linen and purple and silk and scarlet, and every kind of citron wood and every article of ivory and every article made from very costly wood and bronze and iron and marble, 13 and cinnamon and spice and incense and perfume and frankincense and wine and olive oil and fine flour and wheat and cattle and sheep, and cargoes of horses and chariots and slaves and human lives.

The reasons this city called Mystery Babylon could be Mecca are quite plausible.

John saw this city in a wilderness (Revelation 17:3)

Saudi has used oil to control countries and the merchants of these countries have bowed down to her wish because of the supply of oil. Saudi has also pushed the Jihadist agenda with the revenue received from oil.

The biggest shipping lane in the world is the Red Sea, and Mecca sits right on these trade routes. If Mecca is burned, the city can be easily seen from these shipping lanes.

The commodities that are traded are in line with the products purchased by the oil rich kingdom. Human slaves are still bought and sold in this kingdom.

The manner in which the people mourn over the destruction of this place is typically a Middle Eastern custom i.e., throwing sand over their heads in mourning. (Revelation 17:19)

THE CITY OF NEOM IN SAUDI

The kingdom of Saudi is gradually moving away from radical Islam from the last few years. The oil wealth through which the Saudi's pushed their agenda of Wahabi Islam is under threat as the world moves away from its dependance on oil.

This shift from oil has meant that Saudi Arabia needs to look ahead to a future which is weaned of its dependance to oil. The young de facto ruler Prince Salman has begun to restructure the nation. At the center of his plan to modernize the nation is a city called NEOM which is already under construction. He plans to make this the place the most advanced hi tech city in the world. The city will be built using trillions of dollars and the infrastructure planned is unlike anything that the world has seen.

But in order to make this place a reality, Prince Salman knows that the nation will have to put aside the stone age laws of the past and modernize the nation. The laws have been changed considerably in the last few years to accommodate a more liberal society.

Part of the plan is also to do away with almost 90% of the Hadiths. (*Hadiths are explanations and interpretations of Muhammad's living example.*)

This is already causing a great deal of anger in the Muslim world and it stand to reason that the Anti-Christ will target this city as it seen as a deviation from the radical bent of militant Islam.

THE DESTRUCTION OF BABYLON:

God does not destroy Babylon. But God will judge this city which is the epicenter for the Babylonian religion. The rulers who are controlled by Babylon rebel against Babylon and it is they who destroy Babylon.

The identification of the Beast kingdom leads us to the conclusion that the leader would be a propagator of Islam. The question does arise as to why the Beast and his allies destroy this religious city. A little bit of Islamic eschatology will help us in uncovering this fact. According to the Koran and the Hadith, the end would only come when the Islamic Messiah who is called the Mahdi would arrive to rule over the world.

The Mahdi would destroy Mecca and establish his capital from Jerusalem; He will rule over the world and establish the complete domination of Islam.

VICTORY FOR THE LAMB

The Beast and his allies of the ten kings will assemble to destroy the people of God. They will also gang up to fight against the true Messiah Jesus. Jesus will come in a blaze of glory and destroy the armies of the Beast. The Beast and the false prophet will then be cast into the lake of fire.

And I saw the beast and the kings of the earth and their armies assembled to make war against Him who sat on the horse and against His army. (Revelation 19:19)

(REVELATION 17:14)

These will wage war against the Lamb, and the Lamb will overcome them, because He is Lord of lords and King of kings, and those who are with Him are the called and chosen and faithful."

CHAPTER 9

THE FUTURE BATTLES AGAINST ISRAEL

We are living in last days of the age of man. Six thousand years of the history of man has been punctuated with much strife and pain. War and bloodshed have been the hall mark of our time on the planet. But before it all ends and God steps in once and for all, there are major events that will still need to be fulfilled.

THE BATTLE FOR THE MOUNTAINS OF ISRAEL. (EZEKIEL CHAPTERS 36 TO 39)

1. TIMING

It is a detailed prophecy of the invasion of the land of Israel in the end Times. It talks about this happening in the "latter years" (Ezekiel 38:8) and in the "latter days" (Ezekiel 38:16)

EZEKIEL 38:8

After many days you will be summoned; in the latter years you will come into the land that is restored from the sword, whose inhabitants have been gathered from many nations to the mountains of Israel which had been a continual waste; but its people were brought out from the nations, and they are living securely, all of them.

These chapters in the book of Ezekiel starting from 36 to 39 refer to events during our time. The return of the people of Israel to the Promised Land and the prosperity of the nation are in line with Scripture.

The context and setting of the prophecy show Israel as having been scattered to all the nations, but now re gathered to her land and dwelling there as a nation there once again. This only fits the present time after 1948 A.D.

Its timing is also before her national conversion, salvation and final re gathering at the coming of Christ (Ezekiel 29:21-29), and the glories of the Millennium (Ezekiel 40-48).

In fact, the events of this prophecy form part of the series of events that lead to Israel's repentance and the establishment of the Messianic kingdom.

The strong support from the US and its own military victories makes Israel feel safe and secure. This is also the language of Ezekiel who describes Israel dwelling in safety when this invasion happens (Ezekiel 38:8, 11)

IS THIS BATTLE THE SAME AS THE BATTLE OF ARMAGEDDON?

Bible teachers differ on this battle. There are similarities in both the battle of Ezekiel as well as the battle described by John in Revelation 16.

- In both battles, vast armies want to destroy Israel.
- The Lord intervenes and saves Israel in both battles.
- The birds of the air are called for a feast made up of the bodies of mighty men of war and of horses. (Ezekiel 39:17-20), (Revelation 19:17-18)

Some teachers believe that they are two different battles. The "Gog and Magog" war as it is called in the book of Ezekiel happens before the battle of Armageddon. Since the weapons used by the invading armies are used by Israel as fuel for seven years, it is assumed that this battle will happen at least seven years before the battle of Armageddon. (Ezekiel 39:9)

2. SIGNIFICANCE:

It will be one of the major events in world history. It will be one of the major divine interventions ever which will bring about huge changes in the world. It is the 3rd major prophesied event in a sequence of end time events related to Israel.

The first major prophesied event in Israel's latter history was the rebirth of Israel in 1948 A.D. (Matthew 24:32).

This prepared the way for the recapture of Jerusalem in 1967 A.D. (Luke 22:24)

.... Jerusalem will be trampled underfoot by the Gentiles until the times of the Gentiles are fulfilled.

The recapture of the West bank *the Mountains of Israel* is a fulfillment of Ezekiel 34:38.

The next major prophetic event that can be expected is what the Bible calls "The Gog and Magog" war. This will be an invasion of the Mountains of Israel which will be defeated by divine intervention (Ezekiel 38).

3. WHICH ARE THE NATIONS INVOLVED IN THIS INVASION?

EZEKIEL 38:1-2

And the word of the LORD came to me saying, "Son of man, set your face toward Gog of the land of Magog, the prince of Rosh, Meshach and Tubal, and prophesy against him...

GOD speaks to Gog. Gog is a title like Pharaoh, Caesar or Tsar, and it means a mountain, strong ruler or a dictator. Gog is the one who initiates and leads this invasion. But as we read further, we realize that it is God who is mobilizing this war. GOD will use this as an opportunity to judge Gog. So, GOD is ultimately in control.

But Gog has his own evil motivations to invade Israel.

EZEKIEL 38:3-5

'Thus says the Lord GOD, "Behold, I am against you, O Gog, prince of Rosh, Meshech and Tubal.

I will turn you about and put hooks into your jaws, and I will bring you out, and all your army, horses and horsemen, all of them splendidly attired, a great company with buckler and shield, all of them wielding swords; Persia, Ethiopia and Put with them, all of them with shield and helmet; Gomer with all its troops; Beth-togarmah from the remote parts of the north with all its troops—many peoples with you.

Here it is clear that it is God who is bringing these nations against Israel. Sometimes GOD will use Israel as His anvil for justice. God's foreign policy has not changed as far as Israel goes. He has promised to bless those who bless Israel and curse those who curse Israel (Genesis 12:2-3). Nations that come against Israel bring judgment upon themselves.

So let us identify these nations.

Rosh is Russia. Magog is parts of Russia and Central Asia. Meshech and Tubal are in modern day Turkey. Persia is Iran. Cush represents the area south of Egypt which is Sudan. Put represents Libya. Gomer and Togarmah are in Turkey. Ethiopia is also part of this group.

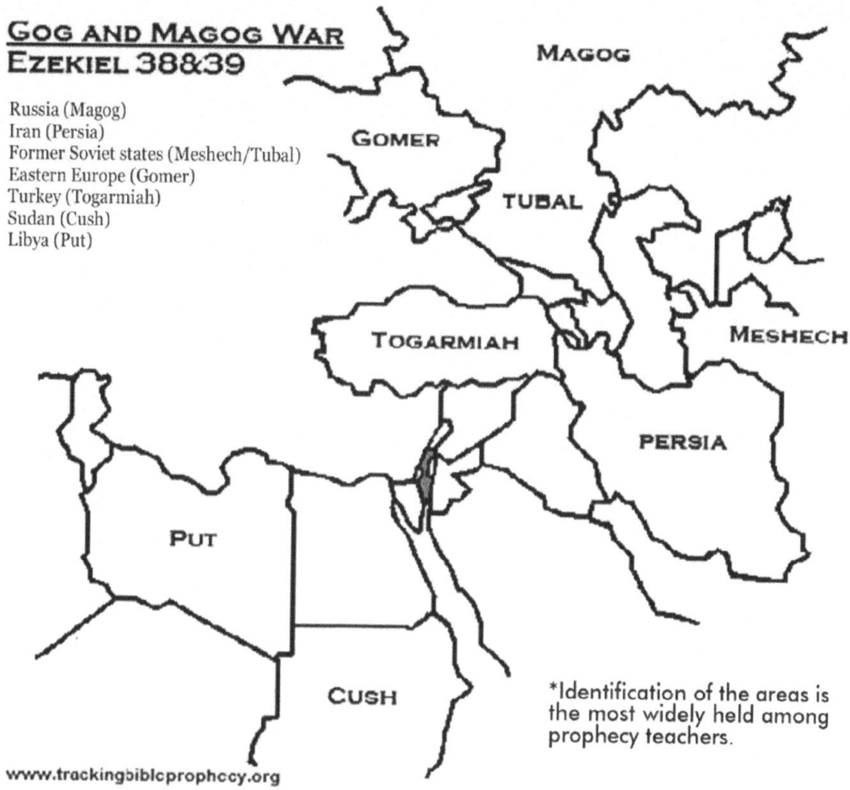

We must bear in mind that the nations mentioned in these passages of scriptures do not have the same boundaries today as they did in Biblical times. But we do have an indication of the general area that these nations are positioned.

Another important factor is that with the exception of Russia, all these nations are Islamic. The former Soviet Union though did have as part of its republic, nations like Azerbaijan, Kazakhstan, Kirghizia, Tajikistan, Turkmenistan, and Uzbekistan. These are Muslim majority nations.

We can already see the partnership of these nations. Russia, Iran and Turkey are allies. Russia will put together a coalition of forces to move against Israel. All the Islamic nations in any case want Israel to be weakened and ultimately destroyed.

EZEKIEL 39:2

I will turn you around, drive you on, take you up from the remotest parts of the north and bring you against the mountains of Israel.

The attack is against the mountains of Israel. Not all of Israel is mountainous. The western part of Israel has the coastal plains. The mountains of Israel are in the West Bank or what the world calls "the occupied territories." This is wrong as it implies that Israel does not have the right to occupy these territories.

The Mountains of Israel are the high ground which is actually the heart of Biblical Israel.

The West bank was captured by Israel in the 1967 war. But all this land was given in a Covenant by GOD to the nation of Israel. The whole earth belongs to God and He has the right to give it to anyone He chooses.

But this has become a controversial topic and the world leaders insist it should be given to the Palestinians. The "Mountains of Israel" have become the center of the controversy. But in the book of Ezekiel, it is God who has decided to give the people of Israel these mountains (Ezekiel 36).

God has made it clear that he has given these mountains to Israel. He has also warned the nations that he will judge those that seek to take this right away from Israel.

This war is not against the entire country of Israel but an attempt to take back the mountains or namely the West Bank. Israel is a nuclear power and, in the situation, where its survival is at stake it will not shy away from using nuclear weapons. It therefore seems unlikely that there would be an invasion of the whole of Israel.

But what Russia and these Nations would calculate is that invading the West Bank would not directly threaten the existence of Israel. The pretext for this invasion will be to enforce the UN Resolutions (like 2334) that say that the West Bank and East Jerusalem does not belong to Israel and her occupation of the West Bank is against International Law.

With the breakdown of peace talks, the settlements in the West bank continue to grow. They could insist that since the peace talks have failed and the settlement activity of the Jews in the West Bank continues unabated, this is a necessary step. Russia's official justification for the invasion will be to solve the Palestinian issue.

They will attempt to establish a Palestinian state on the Mountains of Israel and to impose a two-state solution in accordance with what the world wants. The world wants to divide the land into two parts – one part for the Israelites and the other for the Palestinians.

By limiting the invasion to the West Bank, Russia will know that Israel will not go to a full-scale war against Russia. It would be foolish to go to war with Russia unless her own survival was at stake. This explains why Israel does not defend itself in the prophecy.

Behind these events, Satan has a two-stage plan to destroy Israel.

Stage 1 – Take control of the mountains of Israel in the name of setting up a Palestinian state there. This will greatly weaken Israel's position and her ability to defend herself.

Stage 2 – Wipe Israel out of existence.
The attempt to take the Mountains of Israel by Gog will fail (Ezekiel 38).

God will destroy the enemies on the mountains of Israel. God will do this through natural disasters. The whole world will then know and acknowledge God's power.

EZEKIEL 39:3-5

I will strike your bow from your left hand and dash down your arrows from your right hand. You will fall on the mountains of Israel, you and all your troops and the peoples who are with you; I will give you as food to every kind of predatory bird and beast of the field. You will fall on the open field; for it is I who have spoken," declares the Lord GOD.

THE "ABOMINATION THAT CAUSES DESOLATION"

But where Gog will fail, the "Beast from the Sea" or "The Anti-Christ" will succeed.

MATTHEW 24:15-21

"Therefore, when you see the ABOMINATION OF DESOLATION which was spoken of through Daniel the prophet, standing in the holy place (let the reader understand), then those who are in Judea must flee to the mountains. Whoever is on the housetop must not go down to get the things out that are in his house. Whoever is in the field must not turn back to get his cloak. But woe to those who are pregnant and to those who are nursing babies in those days! But pray that your flight will not be in the winter, or on a Sabbath. For then there will be a great tribulation, such as has not occurred since the beginning of the world until now, nor ever will.

Jesus warned the Jewish people that when they would see the "Abomination of Desolation" in the Holy place, they are to flee to the mountains. The abomination is with regards to the Jewish place of worship. At this time there exists a Mosque at the Holy site. This is the same spot where the first and the second Jewish temple were built.

Many believe that the third Jewish temple will be rebuilt and the Old Testament sacrifices and offerings would begin once again. The Orthodox Jews have never given up their dream to build a temple here once again.

But for this to happen, the Mosque would have to be demolished. This is no ordinary mosque. The Muslims believe that Mohammad was taken up to heaven from this very spot. This is considered the third holiest place for the Muslims. It would take an extra ordinary change of heart for this to take place on the part of the Muslim leadership.

In any case the "Anti-Christ" will take over the mountains of Judea and Samaria including East Jerusalem where the place for the Jewish temple exists. The Jews will then have to flee to the mountains of Jordan.

The invasion of Israel by the Anti-Christ will usher in a time what the

Bible describes as the "great Tribulation". It is a period of three and a half years of terror not only for Israel but for all of God's people who refuse to bow down to the Anti-Christ and worship him. (Revelation 13)

THE BATTLE OF ARMAGEDDON - THE FINAL BATTLE

In the Bible, Armageddon refers to a valley or a plain which runs north west to south east along the foot of Mount Carmel in the north of Israel. This place is also known as the valley of Megiddo. This region was a very important location in Biblical times because it provided a natural gateway through the central mountain regions of Israel. It was also a key connection point between trading routes and nations wanted to control it because of its great strategic importance.

As a result, it was conquered many times. It was conquered by the Egyptians, Canaanites, Philistines, Israelites, Assyrians, Persians, Greeks and the Romans. Many great battles in Israel's history were fought here.

It is here that Gideon and his 300 men defeated the Midianites (Judges 7). It is here that Saul and Jonathan died as they fought against the Philistines (1 Samuel 31). King Josiah died here as he fought against the forces of Pharaoh Neco (2 Kings 23).

We now come to the final battle in history at a place called Armageddon. This place is mentioned in (Revelation 16:16) But the battle that will take place according to this passage is far greater than any battles fought here before.

REVELATION 16:12-14

The sixth angel poured out his bowl on the great river, the Euphrates; and its water was dried up, so that the way would be prepared for the kings from the east.

And I saw coming out of the mouth of the dragon and out of the mouth of the beast and out of the mouth of the false prophet, three unclean spirits like frogs; for they are spirits of demons, performing signs, which go out to the kings of the whole world, to gather them together for the war of the great day of God, the Almighty.

REVELATION 16:15

And they gathered them together to the place which in Hebrew is called Har-Magedon.

The Bible gives us a panoramic view of the final battle that awaits the earth. But this is no ordinary battle. It is instigated by Satan himself. He is the dragon, the serpent of old who throws one final roll of the dice. In his insatiable hatred for God, he has made many attempts to destroy the people of God. Starting from the garden of Eden where he deceived man and took away the dominion given to him by God.

The Beast who has been anointed by Satan for the final attempt to destroy the people of God is alongside him. The False prophet who performs great signs and wonders to deceive the kings of the earth is part of this unholy trinity.

Even the armies of the kings of the whole world are gathered to be a part of this final battle. They have as their leader the "Beast from the Sea."

THE SIXTH TRUMPET—ARMY FROM THE EAST

We learn about this battle from the Trumpets of Revelation also. Remember the seals, trumpets and bowls that the book of Revelation teaches us occur simultaneously.

REVELATION 9:13-16

Then the sixth angel sounded, and I heard a voice from the four horns of the golden altar which is before God, one saying to the sixth angel who had the trumpet, "Release the four angels who are bound at the great river Euphrates." And the four angels, who had been prepared for the hour and day and month and year, were released, so that they would kill a third of mankind. The number of the armies of the horsemen was two hundred million;

Imagine an army of 200 million that goes to war. With our modern weapons, the destruction would be unprecedented. We are given the number of those who die because of this war. A third of mankind will be killed (Revelation 9:18)

It is important that we keep a close watch on world events. In the region around Israel there is a lot of unrest, particularly in Syria, Lebanon and Iraq. The tensions in this region especially with the sudden entrance of ISIS on the world scene took everyone by surprise.

The speed at which the leadership of ISIS took over vast stretches of this region was shocking. What was even more surprising was the fact that thousands of people from different parts of the world went over to the side of ISIS. The Muslim dream of domination over the world through a revived Islamic Caliphate had many Muslims excited.

The Quran and the Hadiths actually advocate this situation. The Muslims are to look forward to a world leader called the "Mahdi" who would be a descendent of Mohammad. He is supposed to bring the complete domination of Islam over the earth.

THE RETURN OF JESUS

The Beast and the false prophet will assemble a huge army of the nations of the earth. But this army is assembled to make war with Jesus. It is in this place a colossal battle will be fought between good and evil. The day of God's wrath has come.

This unique day is given many names in the Bible.

i. The great day of God Almighty - Revelation 16:14

ii. The great day of His wrath - Revelation 6:17

iii. The great and awesome day of the Lord – Joel 2:11, 2:31, Malachi 4:5, Acts 2:20

REVELATION 6:12-17

I looked when He broke the sixth seal, and there was a great earthquake; and the sun became black as sackcloth made of hair, and the whole moon became like blood; and the stars of the sky fell to the earth, as a fig tree casts its unripe figs when shaken by a great wind. The sky was split apart like a scroll when it is rolled up, and every mountain and island were moved out of their places.

Then the kings of the earth and the great men and the commanders and the rich and the strong and every slave and free man hid themselves in the caves and among the rocks of the mountains; and they said to the mountains and to the rocks, "Fall on us and hide us from the presence of Him who sits on the throne, and from the wrath of the Lamb; for the great day of their wrath has come, and who is able to stand?"

God has been very patient with Man. The absolute impunity with which God is blasphemed is horrifying. Many people take the name of Jesus and use it like a cuss word. It is a world in which the good is mocked and evil is glorified.

But this will not carry on for much longer. "The Day of the Lord" approaches rapidly.

This is the day men will tremble at the sight of Jesus. On this day, the pride of man will be humbled and only God will be glorified. The kings of the earth and its mighty men will hide from His presence. In fact, they will call out to the rocks and the mountains to fall on them in order to hide them from the presence of the Creator.

REVELATION 19:11-19

And I saw heaven opened, and behold, a white horse, and He who sat on it is called Faithful and True, and in righteousness He judges and wages war. His eyes are a flame of fire, and on His head are many diadems; and He has a name written on Him which no one knows except Himself.

He is clothed with a robe dipped in blood, and His name is called The Word of God. And the armies which are in heaven, clothed in fine linen, white and clean were following Him on white horses.

And I saw heaven opened, and behold, a white horse, and He who sat on it is called Faithful and true, and in righteousness He judges and wages war.

And I saw the beast and the kings of the earth and their armies assembled to make war against Him who sat on the horse and against His army.

Jesus will defeat the armies of the Beast by a sword that comes out of His mouth, which is His Word. He is the king of kings and the Lord of Lords. The nations of the earth will now meet the true ruler of the earth. The whole earth was made through Him and for Him.

It will be a time of great joy for the people of God, but a time of trouble for those who have rejected His offer of salvation. The Beast and the false prophet will be thrown into the lake of fire. (Revelation 19:20)

REVELATION19:15-16

From His mouth comes a sharp sword, so that with it He may strike down the nations, and He will rule them with a rod of iron; and He treads the wine press of the fierce wrath of God, the Almighty. And on His robe and on His thigh, He has a name written, "KING OF KINGS, AND LORD OF LORDS."

JESUS WARNS THE CHURCH TO BE READY

In the midst of these dramatic events, the Lord gives us a very important warning. The warning is that Jesus will be coming soon and He wants His people to be awake. He will arrive at the time of this battle. God's patience with the evil ways of man is now over. The Lord will come to take over the planet He created.

REVELATION 16:15

"Behold, I am coming like a thief. Blessed is the one who stays awake and keeps his clothes, so that he will not walk about naked and men will not see his shame."

The Lord through the prophets had warned that this day would come. It would be called "The day of the Lord". It would be a day when God would bring down the haughtiness of man. He had warned that His wrath would be poured out on those who had continually rejected the truth and did evil.

Two thousand years ago He came as the "Lamb of God" who took away the sins of the world. But now he would come as the all-conquering king who will establish His righteous rule over the earth.

This was the "Rock" of Daniel Chapter 2.

This rock will become a mountain which fills the whole earth.

The kingdom of God would be established and the righteous ruler would rule.

CHAPTER 10

THE KING RETURNS

The story of humanity has been pretty amazing. God made all things beautiful when he created the Heavens and the Earth. There was fellowship between God and man with perfect harmony between all the creatures made by God. In a perfect world everything was good. There was no sickness and disease and no pain or sorrow or death.

It was the age of innocence.

God gave everything on the earth to Man so that he could have dominion. The only exception was that the decision of what was right and wrong would be the prerogative of God.

It was this temptation to play God that got mankind into trouble. When Adam and Eve ate from the tree of the knowledge of good and evil, in essence, they had moved into territory they should have stayed out of. Mankind has now gone through six thousand years of continuing to play God but with disastrous results.

Every kind of human government has in the end failed Man. Very rarely in history have there been times of peace and prosperity. Injustice and unrighteousness have been the hallmark of the reign of man.

It is to set things right once again that Jesus came as the "Son of Man". He came to restore us back to God by paying the price for our rebellion.

Now Jesus is set to return as the "King of kings".

The world remains largely unmoved by the warnings that God has given to mankind. In an increasingly atheistic world, the Church is called to be awake to the return of the Savior. Jesus has given the church a summary of the things that would happen, once He rose again and went to be seated at the right hand of the Father in Heaven.

For 2000 years the Gospel has been declared to the nations of the earth. The church which began like a mustard seed has now grown to be a large tree. One of the signs that Jesus had given the Church was that the Gospel would be preached to the ends of the earth. And then the end would come.

We are now at that time of the end. What does Jesus expect of His church? How are we to prepare for His return? Jesus has revealed how He wanted the Church to be ready for His return.

1. BE ALERT

MARK 13:33-37

"Take heed, keep on the alert; for you do not know when the appointed time will come. It is like a man away on a journey, who upon leaving his house and putting his slaves in charge, assigning to each one his task, also commanded the doorkeeper to stay on the alert.

Therefore, be on the alert—for you do not know when the master of the house is coming, whether in the evening, at midnight, or when the rooster crows, or in the morning— in case he should come suddenly and find you asleep. What I say to you I say to all, 'Be on the alert!'"

If we work at any job or are in business, we would be diligent as we have accountability towards our employer or our customers. In the same manner we have accountability towards our Lord. Salvation is a gift of God received through faith, but rewards are dependent on our diligence in fulfilling the task given to us by God.

Since we do not know when the Lord will return, it is important to be alert.

2. VALUE THE RELATIONSHIP THAT WE HAVE WITH GOD

In the parable of the ten virgins in (Matthew 25:1-12) we come across five virgins who value the relationship they have with the bridegroom. In every culture especially the Middle Eastern region, the wedding day is the most important day in the life of a girl. There is much preparation that goes into it and the girls and their families go through a lot of excitement as well as anticipation.

But the other five virgins did not understand, and were unprepared for the arrival of the bridegroom. They did not take oil with them and were left behind because they were not ready. Through this parable, Jesus cautions the Church which is His bride to be ready and to look forward to His coming.

3. BE A GOOD STEWARD OF THE TALENTS GIVEN BY GOD

MATTHEW 25:14-15

"For it is just like a man about to go on a journey, who called his own slaves and entrusted his possessions to them. To one he gave five talents, to another, two, and to another, one, each according to his own ability; and he went on his journey.

In the parable of the talents in Matthew 25, the Lord revealed that He has given talents to each of us and expects us to be diligent and faithful in handling them. Being good stewards of the gifts and talents God has given us will bring much reward.

God will reward each one according to their faithfulness in using the talents given by Him. The exciting reality is that Jesus will rule over the earth for a thousand years in a golden period called the Millennium.

The Bible declares that we are the heirs of God and co- heirs with Christ.

The Bible encourages us not to lose hope when we suffer for the sake of the kingdom of God. This life is a preparation for the life to come.

MATTHEW 25:19

"Now after a long time the master of those slaves came and settled accounts with them.

God will take an account from His people and reward each one accordingly.

There is much joy in store for those who have been alert and looking forward to the return of the King.

As the age of man draws to a close and the kngdoms of the world become the kingdom of our God, we have very little time left.

Let's prepare for the coming of our King.

The time of the end draws near....
